From Motorcycles to Machine Guns

The Very Necessary Story of Sgt. Brandon C. Ladner, USMC

Compiled by TM Fitzgerald

DEDICATION

In remembrance of (but not limited to) the warriors who served with the 1/5 Marines on the May 22, 2009 deployment to Afghanistan, and dedicated to all Veterans who've returned from their wars overseas who didn't quite make it all the way home.

-Semper Fidelis.

"Empathy: it's not just about reading someone else's story and being at one with all the characters and events. It's also about feeling the emotions of the main character. Empathy is living life with others with certain mindfulness: observing, listening, and understanding; entering the deep waters of another person's thoughts and experiences..."

-Center for Building Empathy
and Understanding

CONTENTS

-INTRODUCTION-

"It's time for this country to become reacquainted with its military."

Dr. Michael Schoenbaum, Ph.D. and senior advisor for mental health services at The National Institute of Mental Health has stated:

"'This (PTSD epidemic) is more complicated than 'war is hell.' These Veterans did not simply become (anonymous) numbers. They were each somebody's son, husband, brother, father, and friend..."

It was by no coincidence that in September of 2014 journalist and author Brett Gillin scribed the following:

"It's an unfortunate fact that all casualties of war do not happen on the battlefield."

His name wasn't Apollo, wasn't Hercules, or Zeus. His name was not Atlas, though some might agree to say that this man certainly carried the weight of the world upon his shoulders. He wasn't some renowned king, god or otherwise renowned general but who Brandon Charles Ladner was, though, was an extraordinary and stubbornly determined individual. At the same time, Brandon was also the model of a gentleman; a principled, handsome and charismatic man who possessed an energetic and enthusiastically sincere presence: the kind of guy who lived to wring every ounce out of every drop of life. Indisputably, he'd been a hero in the making: one who had willingly (if not eagerly) stepped forward, voluntarily electing to become a Marine and fight for his country: defending the United States against all enemies foreign and domestic.

However, as with previous generations of men who found themselves tending to the overly complicated throes of war, there also came an unwelcome secondary matter of concern: a thinly veiled, virtually hidden undercurrent that would run deep for this Marine and many others like him. It wasn't about the 'good versus evil,' or the 'us versus them' positions that most people think of when they envision unwelcome battles. His was about something else entirely.

From Motorcycles to Machine Guns essentially began as a very broad yet comprehensive collection of facts, statistics, statements and indiscriminate points of view about a very specific condition affecting many of this nation's Veterans: PTSD. Derived from various resources, each scrap of information predictably began painting a bigger picture of one man in particular, a United States Marine whom everybody should take initiative to learn more about. Numerous hearts and voices joined as one, committed to delivering the story of *this* particular Marine to the *rest* of the world. However, it's hoped also, that by sharing *his* story, *his* life, that perhaps *other* lives will be positively affected and other Veteran's families may be spared the heartache of losing one of their own.

From Motorcycles to Machine Guns is the true story of just one (of too many, by the way) Operation Enduring Freedom (OEF) Marine who lost his personal battle with post-traumatic stress disorder (PTSD). On September 9, 2014, nineteen days following his 27th birthday, Marine Sergeant Brandon Ladner became part of a painful statistic. His wasn't the first (and sadly, not the last) casualty in the ensuing war at home that his deployment (with the renowned 1st Battalion, 5th Marine Regiment, 1st Marine Division (AKA the 1/5) suffered after returning from duty overseas.

It seems an obvious statement to make: *"There are two sides to any given conflict."* However, there's an additional component to consider, one that appears tremendously overlooked if not downright ignored. Indeed, there are two sides, but what about all those who get caught or lost somewhere in the middle?

It's certainly not a new concept, rather one that has seemingly made itself most noticeable after all the obvious battles have long been fought. Recognized as far back to the days of the Civil War, it's an issue that's been swept under rugs for centuries, treated with an indifference that has led the majority of the world to the stand it continues to take today. It's called post-traumatic stress disorder (PTSD), a very real and seriously under-addressed element of war.

If in reading this man's story anybody feels motivated to proclaim, 'Hey! *We were there, too!*' or '*What about women?*' or '*What about this, that, or anything else?*' then perhaps this is the wrong read for you. A point being made clear from the start, political correctness and broad objectivity were *not* driving concerns here. The primary focus of *From Motorcycles to Machine Guns* was meant solely to be about Brandon Charles Ladner's life: one very specific *man*, who incidentally happened to be a United States Marine.

In addition to the much larger problem affecting the *entire* military, Sergeant Ladner (and unfortunately, a statistically large number of his Marine brothers from the same deployment) became part of the existing digit that once came to define the average number of military suicides that took place on a daily basis: twenty-two, a number that doesn't remain static. Its accuracy is controversial as far as reporting the *true* number of deaths that have taken place among Veterans in their own country by their *own* hand.

This Marine's story has been documented for several reasons: the first, to share the existence of and offer an ever so slight glimpse into the life and times of just one of the many who have fallen to the effects of PTSD. The second reason was as an attempt to raise awareness of a problem tormenting so many American military Veterans; men and women alike.

This book was not meant to rewrite history or rework old data. To reiterate, it was meant first to share with the world the story of an extraordinary man who could no longer tell his own and secondly, to remind the world that PTSD is still a subject that needs to be contended with.

To bring a better understanding and awareness to the demon called post-traumatic stress, Brandon's book and everything in it were meant to share not only the life that *he* lived, but sadly the way that he left this world. This book may stir some controversy in its own right simply by the nature of the subject matter involved, and that's okay, but no other explanation or apologies are being offered. The English writer William Hazlitt once stated, "*When something ceases to be a subject of controversy, it ceases to be a subject of interest.*" We can't afford to lose interest in something affecting so many.

As the saying goes, '*Still waters run deep.*' No matter how blistering the temperatures may turn or how inviting it may first appear, no practical person in this world would sensibly consider diving headlong into any body of water without first knowing how deep the water was. Ideally, a person is going to take a good look around first; check out the terrain, learn more about that body of water before wading out, much less impulsively diving into the deep. It's comparable to picking up a biography, especially a military-themed one: you can't feel comfortable in completely losing yourself in another person's story without first getting to know who he or she was from the start. Ideally, you want to look around a little, take in the landscape and see how deep the water is potentially going to get.

From Motorcycles to Machine Guns has been formatted such as it has for several reasons. Keep in mind the following fact: less than ten percent of the American population has accomplished service in the military while even less than that have done so as Marines. Because of that fact in particular, it was necessary to share other, rather wide-ranging information: necessary because, if for nothing else, it was to show the world just how deep the water ran before they dove into this particular Marine's life. (Necessary because the military certainly isn't going to draw attention to anything that could affect recruitment or retention.)

For a vast majority, certain information and side-explanations included herein are what editors would call 'backstory.' (It's the same stuff that some prior military might call 'no-brainers.') No matter what side of the fence you are reading this biographical account from, all such explanations were essential in telling Brandon's story.

If in reading this Marine's account certain information or phrases seem vaguely familiar or you develop the sense or feeling like you've read them someplace before, chances are pretty good that you well may have. Whenever stories (factual accounts especially) about members of the military are put to paper, it's inevitable that certain qualities and characteristics will get repeated. This truth is particularly recognizable when the subject matter is a Marine. Brandon Charles Ladner was one of the few and the proud, one whose story was written to be shared with those who never had the opportunity to meet him: civilian and military alike.

Those who were personally acquainted with Brandon already had the advantage of thoroughly knowing his background, his history, and all the subtle (and not so subtle) nuances that made him who he was. Those people are the lucky ones. Brandon gave all of them a gift: memories, and as the saying goes, "Memories are reminders that we have truly lived."

Perhaps in turning these pages, some of those same people may deliberate how this book about their son, their brother, or friend should have or could have been constructed differently. Some may even determine that we should have mentioned 'this' and others may think we should have included 'that,' but we also need to remember the most important thing: *From Motorcycles to Machine Guns* was compiled to honor Brandon's life, to share with the rest of the world the fact that this man certainly did exist. Shouldn't the world be reminded about *this* Marine? Shouldn't the world know that he lived?

If curiosity is getting the best of you and you want to know how and why such an assorted collection of people pulled together to tell Brandon Ladner's story, then you may want to read the last chapter first. Otherwise, this book appropriately begins with Sgt. Ladner's existence before he chose to become a United States Marine and then continues in sharing the striking effect his life had (and still has) on so many today.

"The goal isn't to live forever. The goal is to create something that will."

It was a unique challenge to pull Brandon Ladner's story together. Long before he chose to become a United States Marine, Ladner was already an individual whom many in this world would have undoubtedly labeled an ideal role model. When asked to describe Brandon, the list of adjectives people used was wide-ranging, as could be expected but in sharing their individual answers, there was also a common element. Nobody ever struggled to find 'just the right words.' Each person defined Ladner with absolute confidence; every word ultimately painting a bigger picture of who Brandon Charles Ladner was and what exactly he meant to them.

TM Fitzgerald

1 -ON YOUR MARK-

"If there be any truer measure of a man than by what he does, it must be by what he gives."

- Robert South

By more than one account, Brandon Ladner was described as good-looking, expressive, gregarious, suave, sociable, outgoing, head-strong, stubborn, undeniably charming, chivalrous, respectful, positive, humble: in short, the absolute last person anyone who was part of his world *ever* thought would become one of a very somber figure. At the end of 2015, that figure, a statistic that was holding at a debatable (and deplorable) twenty-two, signified the average number of Veterans in the United States who commit suicide *each day*. That equated to approximately 154 a week, 616 a month, and over 7,300 lives a year. Obviously, the effects of war disturb a body much deeper than what's visible on the surface.

"You may hate the war, but never hate the ones that fight for they do not choose when or where to fight. All they chose was to protect who they love and even the people they didn't know."

-Millie

There's no risk in reading about this Marine. The risk is in missing the opportunity to learn about and love yet another hero the world is so desperately in need of today. Brandon Ladner lived oblivious to the fact that something was different in the world simply by his ever being here, by his very existence. He had no idea that he would be so remembered.

Although Brandon Ladner was a *Marine*, (not a soldier, and there *is* a difference) these words by Charles Province sum up beautifully why we, as a nation, should give more thought to this country's military as a whole.

"It is the *Soldier*, not the minister
who has given us freedom of religion.
It is the *Soldier*, not the reporter
who has given us freedom of the press.
It is the *Soldier*, not the poet
who has given us freedom of speech.
It is the *Soldier*, not the campus organizer
who has given us freedom to protest.
It is the *Soldier*, not the lawyer
who has given us the right to a fair trial.
It is the *Soldier*, not the politician
who has given us the right to vote.
It is the *Soldier*, who salutes the flag,
who serves beneath the flag,
and whose coffin is draped by the flag,
who allows the protester to burn the flag."

— Charles M. Province

"I have to insist. You *must* read this! You *have* to know this boy; this man, this son, this brother, this MARINE..."

-DW, Former Navy Corpsman

You might never have known about this young man
Brandon Charles Ladner, USMC had he not died.
(And too soon, by the way: as if there's ever a time we could be okay with the loss of any of those we love.)
How often have we heard (or maybe even whispered to ourselves) these words about somebody;
"At least he lived a full life."
Sergeant Ladner did exactly that: he lived a full life, except his time was simply too short. (Understatement of the year, perhaps; "too short.")
Yes, that's right: a sergeant.
In the Marines.
"A damn good-looking one, too!" his mother would proudly tell you (and rightly so.)
He was a fine Marine: outstanding even.
Professional, loyal and proud.
Squared-away: the 'spit-and-polish' kind of Marine fit for a recruiting poster.
But most definitely proud.
Brandon Ladner lived his life to its fullest.
Already, his was one full of dreams that had come true, full of memories many of us spend an entire lifetime to build: built with his own hands.
Dreams, disappointment, rewards, accomplishments, girls – (*the* girl; at least for him.)
He'd even perfected the art of riding motorcycles. (And it *is* an art, you know.)
Brandon had it all.
He was the type of Marine whom others found themselves wanting to be.
He had his friends, his family and, as is the case with all Marines, the line between blood and family he had in his battle-buddy Marines? It was a fine one; sometimes indistinguishable. And Marines know it's like that.

You find your example; a kind of blueprint for the kind of Marine you wish to become. You emulate that example and build yourself up. You build your Marine as you wish to be: only better. It's like that; and to others, Brandon was that Marine.

To others still, - even to the non-Marines in his life, Brandon was still like that.

It would have surprised no one to hear a nephew say to buddies of his own,

"See that guy over there? That's my Uncle Brandon. Yeah, that guy. I want to be just like him."

Because Brandon Ladner was, well he was just *that* type of guy.

He was *that* type of Marine.

He was America's boy.

His life was full. His life was beautiful.

He seemed content, his world complete.

Others envied him and in the most simplistic deception,

His life was beautiful.

Or was it?

Until he was alone.

In a crowd, with family or with friends, he still walked in a darkness, an abyss waiting under each step he took.

Surrounded by love of unmeasurable quantity, the void still kept him company.

No one knew how his smile was strained; painted on each day.

Oh, for some, he'd allowed the walls to crack,

And to select few, he whispered of his demons, perhaps.

But even to those chosen few, he kept quiet of the alarm that began to sound:

The battle within himself.

The same alarm brother (and sister) Veterans may hear,

Perhaps even in reading this now. You know: that alarm.

But Brandon tried to keep his hidden.

He'd convinced himself (and those around him) that his life, his world was okay.

It was anything but-

And America? She slept right through his battle.

Foolishly, arrogantly (and most certainly) his country failed him.

His country failed to save him.

Not his mother, his father family.

Not his best friends or his battle brothers: especially not them.
The number stands at 8,300-8,500 souls a year.
Brothers, sisters, daughters and sons, mothers and fathers alike,
They *all* die.
Brandon Ladner became one of them: the souls of over twenty-two Veterans (including at least one active-duty service member) dying each day.
Every day.
Every day of the year, one falls approximately *every* hour.
And remember,
Brandon was a Marine's Marine.
A late casualty of a war that still raged in his soul.
That war, the war within?
America claimed she had no idea.

"We've refused to hear the cry. In truth, we as a country have refused to hear their cries and have ignored taking care of our own. I ask you, the reader to get to know this Marine: an individual who lived and loved life. This boy I speak of; *this* boy many tell of – he lived, and you will love him. He was a boy who loved motorcycles, who loved life and then grew up and perhaps saved a life or two (or more) as a Marine, and became a man who many could not help but love. Love his life, his spirit, his soul. Love his eyes, his hands, and heart. This book will help you come to know and love the remarkable man *that* boy became. So yes, know him and love him, as I have come to do, but also hate his demon, as do I."
DW, USN

Sgt. Brandon C. Ladner
August 21, 1987 - September 09, 2014

"Memories: a way of holding on to the things you love, the things you are, and the things you never want to lose."

-Kevin Arnold
The Wonder Years

2
-A MOTHER'S LOVE-
"You will always be, because I will always remember you."

Some people may choose to debate that Brandon Charles Ladner's story began after he joined the military and earned his title of Marine but in fact, the story of this Marine began long before he repeated these familiar words:

"I, Brandon Charles Ladner do solemnly swear that I will support and defend the Constitution of the United States against all enemies foreign and domestic..."

Born in Gulfport, Mississippi August 21, 1987, Brandon Ladner was the third child born to Renee and Michael C. Ladner.

"The order of my children's birth wound up being just as I had hoped. I'd wanted two boys and a sweet little girl in the middle. That way, our daughter would have an older and younger brother to take care of her." Renee laughed. "Let me just say they *all* took care of each other, but when Nicole came along, she ended up being very protective of both her brothers."

How did you decide upon Brandon's name?
"I'd already had my first child, Chris. I'd liked the name Brandon, but when Chris was born with all his blond hair, he just struck me as a 'Chris.' So I'd decided if our next baby were a boy, we'd name him Brandon. We'd also thought about Bailey as a name, but Brandon was the name that really stuck in my mind."

"As far as knowing the sex of our children, we didn't know what we were having until the day they were each born. Ultrasounds were not as common to just go and have done back when I had children, at least not like they seem to do them these days. When we were expecting the latest bundle of joy, we had no idea what it was going to be. When Brandon was born, he weighed in at 9lbs 10 oz. and was 21 inches long. He had a head full of beautiful, dark hair and just looked like a Brandon to me."

"He was such a beautiful, chubby, baby. I remember the joy and excitement their daddy had as he went running down to the gift shop. He purchased cigars announcing, 'It's a Boy' to pass around to the family and friends who'd been waiting so patiently to find out what our newest addition was going to be. People don't do that anymore. Most expectant parents these days get the ultrasound so they'll know the sex of their baby before the child is ever born."

"Brandon's big brother Christopher and big sister Nicole loved and adored their new baby brother. Brandon and Chris got along well, and Nicole always wanted to help me take care of him. She loved holding Brandon and giving him his bottle just like he was her very own baby doll. I have to say, there was never a dull moment in the house after Brandon was born. He was so funny, even as a toddler." Renee paused, "And although they sure had their share of moments, particularly through elementary school, Brandon and Nicole ended up being two peas in a pod. They were two-of-a-kind."

"When Brandon was in the fourth grade, we met the Lipsey's: Bob and his children Beau and Breaze. Bob was a single parent, as was I. (My kids and I had moved to Pelham, Alabama about a year before meeting the Lipsey's.) Our girls were only six months apart in age, and our youngest boys were three months apart. We all lived in the same neighborhood, and the kids attended school together. Nicole and Breaze became great friends and so did the boys."

"Bob Lipsey loved Alabama sports, particularly football (and to this day attends all of the home games.) On many occasions, Bob would call the house and ask if my kids could go along with him and his to a game in Tuscaloosa or wherever Alabama happened to be playing that week. As I've said, he and I were both single parents at the time and since he'd asked about the kids going along for games, he eventually asked if I'd like to go to one." Renee giggled, "And what single-woman in her right mind would pass up an offer from such a polite, handsome, man? Without any hesitation, I happily accepted."

"As time passed, Bob and I grew close. Before we knew it, we'd started walking together a few days a week, going out at five-thirty in the morning. Five-thirty was early for me, but I wasn't going to pass up walking with him through the neighborhood. (Eventually, Bob purchased a membership for me at his gym.) Before we knew it, an entire year had passed and we'd fallen in love. Bob asked me to marry him and on Valentine's Day that year, we married, including all our kids in the ceremony."

"Chris, Nicole, and Brandon adored Bob. The kids got along great. It was amazing to watch everybody grow together as a family. The only sibling rivalry that ever happened was between Brandon and Nicole. Like I've said, those two were so much alike. Every one of the kids had very distinct personalities, so there was *always* something going on in the house, particularly with Brandon who ultimately became known as 'the life of the party.'"

"Back when Brandon started school in Mississippi, I remember being so worried about leaving him on his first day. Up to that point, he'd never wanted to be away from me. He was a 'mama's boy'. I loved his clinginess and the bond that he and I shared from day one. As things turned out, he loved getting on the school bus with his friends and siblings and making everybody laugh. Even back then, Brandon loved meeting different people and making new friends. Everybody knew when Brandon Ladner was around."

"Brandon loved school and was such a good student. All the teachers loved him and his big personality, something that Brandon carried all through his life. He made friends with every person he met, young and old alike. I don't believe there was ever a shy bone in that child's body. He had such an affectionate disposition as a child; he'd steal your heart from the get-go. He was the happiest, funniest, little boy you could ever hope to meet. Brandon was also one of the biggest pranksters and enjoyed scaring everybody every chance he could. He loved getting reactions out of people, and boy, could he ever. We could always count on Brandon for a good laugh and a huge smile no matter what the occasion was."

"While growing up and attending elementary and middle school, Brandon played football for six years. When we moved to Alabaster, he decided not to continue playing because he didn't particularly like his new school. That was when he decided to take up riding dirt bikes."

"Bob had made a deal with Brandon that if he got himself a job and saved the money, he'd co-sign with him to buy a new YZ-250 two-stroke Yamaha motorbike. So, that's exactly what Brandon did. When he turned fifteen, Brandon and his step-brother Beau both got themselves jobs at the local grocery store and Brandon saved every dime he made that following year. Bob kept his end of the bargain and got Brandon the bike."

"I'll never forget the day we all went to the shop and he picked out that Yamaha. I don't think I'd ever seen Brandon more excited. I started worrying, though, when I saw how big and tall the bike was. My own feet didn't even touch the ground when I sat on it so of course, I started wondering how my little boy was going to handle this powerful machine, but Brandon did it. Even though he'd taken a rider's safety class before we let him venture off on his own, he still managed a few obligatory scrapes and bruises but never suffered any serious injuries."

"For weeks after buying that thing, he'd wake up every morning saying, 'Oh my God. I can't believe I got the bike I wanted.' He started out big, never wanting any of the smaller bikes. That Yamaha was a powerful bike for such a young man, one who'd never even owned a bike before but Brandon was a big boy, and handled that two-stroke well. I was still a nervous wreck every time he went off on that thing."

"Brandon had bought himself an entire outfit that matched the bike. He looked like a pro riding that thing. There were a few times he came home in the back of a police car because he'd been caught riding up the powerline or through some neighborhood on his way to see one of his buddies but he was a great rider. He respected his bike and knew how quickly he could lose control or get seriously hurt. Even so, he still loved jumping ramps and hills. He'd even taken me out riding a few times and scared the hell out of me. (I didn't know whether to laugh or cry.) He was my little dare-devil."

"Brandon was such a responsible kid, but sometimes he'd get a wild hair and do something that even he never expected. I remember one time he wanted to borrow his brother's car to see a friend. I told him he could use it so long as he was careful and didn't stay at his friend's house too long. The problem was, without asking or telling me the change in his original plans, Brandon decided to go visit the shooting range a few miles down the road in Helena."

"We'd had a big rain the night before but there went Brandon, alone in the car, down this dirt road. As luck would have it, he ended up getting the car stuck in the mud. He hadn't carried his cell phone with him and knew it was a long walk back to civilization to try finding a phone so he took matters into his own hands. The key ended up getting stuck in the ignition, and when he tried pulling it out, it ended up breaking off in the ignition."

"I know he hated the thought of calling to tell me what he had done by getting his brother's car stuck in the mud. (He'd tell me later that he was sweating bullets.) That little spontaneous trip of his cost us almost six-hundred dollars. The car had to be towed, and we had to have a new ignition switch put in. Brandon learned a valuable lesson that day."

"I remember another time; most of the family was sitting in the living room watching television while Brandon and a friend were hanging out in his room. We were all sitting out there when we suddenly heard a loud bang come from Brandon's room. Brandon started yelling in a loud panic, so of course, I ran back and opened the door. The look on those two boys faces was like, 'Oh Lord. We're in trouble now.'"

"'There was Brandon, lying on his bed holding onto his leg and laughing almost hysterically. He was obviously in pain but was trying so hard not to cry in front of his friend. I asked them what happened and Brandon informed me that he'd shot his BB gun at the closet and the shot ricocheted and hit him in the leg. So off to the emergency room we went. The hospital checked him out and eventually told us that cutting the BB out would do more damage than good, so they ended up just leaving it."

"Here's an interesting detail people may not know about him. Brandon never felt compelled to put any tattoos on his body. I mean, he was a Marine, right? Lots of people seem to think that tattoos and Marines go together like peanut butter and jelly." Renee laughed. "He was a man who thought a great deal about his personal appearance." Renee stifled a laugh as in afterthought she added, "He sure spent a lot of money on that hair gel. If you ever saw Brandon without his hair styled and spiked and his beard all neatly groomed, you knew something was wrong."

"Brandon married his high school sweetheart Ashley Seal right out of boot camp. He'd received orders and had to go to California, so he decided to sell his dirt bike. (I hated to see him sell it because I knew he'd miss it.) Ashley and Brandon moved to California and lived off base. That's when they met another Marine, Cole Wilson who was in the same battalion as Brandon. Cole and Brandon became instant best friends and decided they'd all be roommates. Those two had more fun than any two people I've ever known. Even after they both were discharged from the Marines, they remained the best of friends right up to the day Brandon died."

"Despite how outgoing and lively he was, Brandon was, in fact, a *very* private person. He never wanted anybody to know how he truly felt inside. I can't describe it. I mean, on the outside, my boy was always the life of the party. He was the guy who'd be first to arrive and the last to leave. He'd come help set things up then stay overnight or at least come back early the next morning to help clean up the mess and take out the trash. That's just the type of person he was." Renee sighed.

"Brandon had his entire life ahead of him. I still grieve so hard for my baby. He was the most loving, giving, funny, intelligent son and friend that anyone could ask for." After a long pause, Renee softly added, "I'll never understand any of this. I never suspected he was so troubled."

"As far as education went, school was very important to him. Brandon loved acquiring knowledge. He'd already obtained his associate's degree and had been accepted into nursing school. After a lot of hard work and achieving/maintaining his 4.0 GPA, he decided nursing wasn't for him. He said he wanted to make a difference, so he switched majors and started studying Healthcare Management. I mean, imagine that? Brandon said he wanted to go back to school, get his Bachelor's and reenlist in the Marines as an officer then go work in the Veteran's Administration. He wanted to make a difference for our Veterans."

"Brandon loved hanging out with his friends. One of his favorite things to do was build big bonfires and invite as many people as he could find." Pausing in deep thought, Renee continued. "There was so much more to him than just appearances, though. He loved to go tubing down the river, going out to the shooting range, or just hanging out on the beach." Renee paused. "He was always doing something and the more people he had around him, the better."

"There wasn't too much Brandon *didn't* like. I mean, he disliked mean people, didn't like anybody cursing in front of his Mama," Renee paused to take a breath. "-or fussy people. Brandon didn't like for people to fuss. The thing is, though, once you were around him for any length of time, you wouldn't be in a fussy mood. His personality was that infectious."

When asked to describe her son's general outlook on life, Renee began listing attributes, the characteristics that others would come to know Brandon Ladner by. "As a child, he was the funniest, and most adventurous little boy I ever knew. He always played well with others, and if nobody else was around, he could also occupy himself just fine. Even in his earlier days, Brandon preferred surrounding himself with people. He was always spontaneous. That's just who he was," With a catch in her breath, Renee paused and abruptly switched gears. "-and you know what else? He loved to sing, (later in life, he enjoyed doing this rap thing called freestyling with his buddies) and cook. Brandon loved to cook."

"Brandon and I were *always* close. As I've said before, he was a true mama's boy and thrived on the attention. He'd always come to me when he needed advice or when he was upset about something. Even as he got older, he always wanted me to come along and hang out with him and his friends. He made me feel like I'd done something right while he was growing up."

"While I was proud when Brandon joined the Marines, at the same time, it proved to be very distressing for me. He'd first talked about going into the military sometime around his freshman year of high school. When he hit junior year, he reminded me again how he wanted to be a Marine. He came home one day and talked about enlisting. *'Mom, I want to join the Marines.'* I think he was influenced by my son-in-law TJ and his friend Doug Sinclair because they were both already Marines," Renee paused. "-In fact, Doug was the one who went with Nicole, and the two of them took Brandon to the recruiting office."

"Being only seventeen at the time, Brandon enlisted under the Marine's delayed entry program. After all the paperwork had been completed, he asked me how I felt about it." Renee paused again as she thought about her next words. "I wasn't happy at first, but I wasn't about to be the one to discourage him from pursuing his dreams. I told him that I wouldn't have chosen the Marines as an occupation, but if that was what he wanted, then he had my approval. I knew there'd be all kinds of opportunities for him to travel and further his education. (Education was what Brandon was all about and he certainly took advantage of that aspect.) I knew the Marines would help him achieve all his goals so I gave him my blessing. I knew he'd make an excellent Marine."

"It wasn't just about me giving blessings and support. His dad and step-dad also wanted the best for him as well but I was 'Mom.' He was my baby. When he left for boot camp and initial training, I knew he was going to be gone for a long time. We'd never been apart from each other like that. My little boy was going away and becoming a man. I didn't want him to leave. That wasn't all I was dealing with at the time, either."

"Brandon's sister Nicole had joined the Air Force around the same time he enlisted in the Marines. They were both in boot camp at the same time, literally hundreds of miles away from home. My only girl was in San Antonio, and my youngest had left for Parris Island. My two youngest children had stepped up and were making lives for themselves in the military."

"Brandon had been a tough little boy all his life. I knew he'd be okay. Nicole though, she was our little diva. I just couldn't imagine her training in that Texas heat every day but she did it." Renee shared a nervous laugh. "My heart was a mess. I worried so much about both of them, but they were each so independent. I should've known I didn't have anything to worry about with either one of them."

On June 06, 2006, seventeen-year-old Brandon Ladner enlisted in the United States Marine Corps. He had long aspired to become a Marine and dutifully earned the coveted eagle, globe, and anchor. Brandon fulfilled his military obligation and eventually returned home safe and sound. Nobody realized that wasn't entirely true. Brandon had not returned the same person he had left, but it would be several years before anybody knew. When he came home, nightmares and depression accompanied him.

"Brandon completed basic training at Parris Island in September of 2006 and I remember it was hot as hell in Carolina. I guess this may seem a peculiar thing for a mother to say, (though it's the truth) but when we first saw him, he was extremely buff. I mean,

Brandon had lost a lot of weight and looked fantastic. Happy that basic training was finally over, he was eagerly looking forward to his first duty station. We were *all* tremendously proud of him."

"He went to Kuwait on his first overseas deployment, and everything went off fine, but when they deployed to Afghanistan, I had a lot of mixed feelings about that. Many Marines had already died over there so of course, I was worried. We'd talked all about that and Brandon continuously reassured me, telling me that everything was going to be just fine."

"We weren't able to keep in touch with one another much once he deployed though and oh how I hated that. At the time he was over there, they weren't getting mail but maybe once a month. In fact, there was some mail he never got at all. That was tough. I hated the thought, the possibility of getting that knock at the door. You know the one. When your child is in an active war zone, you *have* to think about that, the possibilities. You pray it never happens, but you never know."

After Brandon's deployment to Afghanistan concluded, Renee was beyond thrilled when he returned home, all limbs and abilities intact. She never suspected there was anything else to worry about. Ladner was honorably discharged from active duty, began looking for a job, started college, and aspired to change the world. Brandon secured a respectable civil service position. When he started college, he went on to achieve and maintain a 4.0 GPA, eventually switching majors so that his education would better prepare him for his goal of making changes in the troubled VA system. It was all part of his plan to change the world.

As far as bridging the gap between Marine and civilian life (transitioning), from all outward appearances, it appeared that Brandon had made his way back into the civilian world without any problem. Nobody saw it at the time, but apparently, that was not the case. Though he'd never completely shown it, at some point after stepping away from his role of an active-duty Marine, circumstances in Brandon Ladner's life ceased to fall into the realm of ordinary and instead turned unfamiliar. The always positive, smiling Brandon knew he had fallen into a place he didn't want to be. It wasn't anywhere he had ever been and he, himself couldn't figure out exactly what was wrong. All anybody else knew was that something had changed in Brandon and not in a good way.

"Brandon always wanted to shine, always wanted to make people laugh. He was truly a man with big goals and a huge heart. I don't know how this PTSD so completely consumed him. It left such a huge void in his life after he returned from Afghanistan." Renee paused. "He never let anybody see it for what it was."

When asked to describe her son, Renee smiled and shook her head slowly. "I don't even know where to begin. There are so many things I can tell you." After being encouraged to speak whatever was on her mind, this Marine's proud mother began describing Brandon. "From the start, it seemed that he was going to be a different kind of child. He was always a bit of a shaker and a mover. I say that because whatever goals he'd set for himself, he'd work hard and always achieve them."

Renee closed her eyes, searching her mind. "Brandon was very aware of the people in his life. He looked up to and deeply respected his male role-models. He knew what he wanted and always strived to make everybody proud and never wanted to disappoint. Brandon led a very disciplined existence at times and an amazing person." Renee stopped as another thought suddenly came to mind. "My boy was always concerned for others, you know, with how they were doing, how they felt. It was never just for show. He'd ask how you were and honestly cared about your response."

"Brandon was outrageously funny, and it sure didn't hurt that he was handsome and smart as a whip, too. Brandon was *always* respectful of others and loved people. He cared about how he looked and about what other people thought of him," Renee paused before adding, "-that was *always* important to Brandon, how others thought of him. It wasn't that he was vain or full of himself; he just took pride in his appearance. He always wanted to make a good impression."

"One thing that Brandon especially enjoyed doing was building bonfires and gathering all his friends together for parties. Jamy Wayman would bring his guitar and play for their friends." Renee paused in thought as she continued. "Brandon had many talents. Though he never took a big interest in actually learning how, Brandon could play the piano a little bit. Most people never knew this. He could also pick a few songs on the guitar, too but probably the best talent that everybody knew about him was how he could do this thing called 'free-styling' which is just spontaneous rapping. He kept his friends entertained, that's for sure."

"You have to understand, throughout his entire life, Brandon had *always* been very people-oriented. He loved being around others and never liked being alone. He'd always been so positive and happy all the time. It was hard for me to fathom how anything could upset that. Of course, I'd suspected something in him had changed but just chalked it up to being girl problems." Renee stopped. "That seems so easy to say in retrospect. I should have recognized it was more than that. I guess he'd expressed his frustrations when having to deal with some issues when he talked with other Marines, you know, like some of his battle buddies but Brandon never discussed any of that with me. He never wanted me to worry about anything. I know things that happened in Afghanistan were still weighing heavy on his mind."

Renee took a deep breath before she could continue. Her voice softened as she explained her son's life. "During Brandon's last few months, whenever I'd ask how he was doing, he'd always say, *'It's just a slump, Mama. I need to work through this myself.'* Despite being such an outgoing person, my son was private and being such, Brandon never allowed anybody to help him, and I never pushed." Renee's voice fell quiet. "I should have pushed." With tears welling in her eyes, Renee concluded, "I just didn't know what was happening to my son."

"In his last few months, several friends of his knew *something* wasn't quite up to par, but the fact of the matter is, nobody realized just how bad things were. Nobody knew what exactly PTSD was. It wasn't until sometime around the beginning of August I think, after he shared one peculiar post or another on Facebook that made a lot of people step forward and ask what was going on, if he was okay. That was the first time I suspected that something was wrong."

"Brandon had withdrawn from everybody. He wouldn't return calls, wouldn't go out, nothing. Before the whole PTSD situation crept in, he'd always maintained the most awesome and amazing friendships with everybody in his life. He never wanted me to know when things were bothering him because he didn't want me to worry. Up until about two months before he passed away, he'd call his buddies or go out with them for a beer or talk but after he returned from his deployment, something changed all that."

"I believe the happiest moments in Brandon's life were when he had all his family and friends together. If he ever thought or saw anybody was feeling down or out of sorts, he'd do everything he could to cheer them up. I never knew anything about the 'twenty-two a day' until the tragedy struck our family."

"Marines don't typically ask for help. They think it makes them look weak. I think the VA or the military itself needs to do more to help our vets when they return from war. I think more educating about PTSD and the potential effects of war need to be addressed. There needs to be more studies about why these men (and women) are struggling so badly when they come back. I think fewer lives would be lost if more was done *prior* to deployment."

"Brandon had no idea as to why he was struggling. He knew he had a lot going on mentally, but he didn't know what to do. He felt like he was the only one suffering those things. He eventually expressed to a few of his Marine buddies that he was battling survivor's guilt." Renee took a breath, tears filling her eyes. "I look back and can see that Brandon clearly had all the signs. I wish I'd known more about PTSD. I could have helped him."

"I know I've posted a lot on-line about Brandon since losing him, but it's been my way of expressing one of the biggest sorrows I'll ever carry. Losing my youngest child has left a huge void in my life. No matter how any mother loses a child, there is no bigger heartache she will ever face; I don't care what anybody says. Talking about my Brandon helps comfort my soul. I'll never stop grieving for my precious child."

"I thank God I still have my two beautiful children and two adorable grandsons to share my love with. They've all brought happiness back to my heart. Time hasn't made Brandon's loss any easier, but with all the love, compassion, and support I've received from friends and so many people I never knew, I've been able to cope. It'll soon be two years and each day is just as hard as the last."

"All the while he was growing up, Brandon was the kind of child that anybody would be proud to call their own. He was always so willing to help others, so genuinely caring about everything. That's why his behavior during his last few months was such a shock. He seemed to have withdrawn from everybody." Renee paused. "I didn't know it at the time, but he was exhibiting classic signs of PTSD."

December 2015: *"I miss his smile, his laughter, his jokes, his big bear hugs, and his explosive personality. I miss everything about him, my 'Little Moe.' I drive to his resting place every day to tell him how much he's loved and missed. The only light out there (other than the office) are his Christmas tree lights. He knows how much his mama loves him."*

"My boy had such a big heart and the personality to match. He had so much fun in his lifetime. I want other people to know what a great person he was.

TM Fitzgerald

3 -NICOLE HARRIS-

"To choose only one quality to describe my brother is difficult because he possessed so many great ones."

There's an old Vietnamese proverb that states "Brothers and sisters are as close as hands and feet." Every relationship a person may experience in life is unique in its own way, but the bond that brothers and sisters share is different. As a matter of fact, this bond is so significant that in the Hindu religion, there's actually a yearly festival celebrating it called *Raksha Bandhan.*

In India, *Raksha Bandhan* is celebrated on the full-moon day of the Hindu month of Shravana (August). "The frail thread of Rakhi is considered stronger than iron chains as it binds the most beautiful relationship (of siblings) in an inseparable bond of love and trust."

Siblings: initially the bane of *every* child's existence, are one another's 'go-to' resource for all those SHTF scenarios that parents only learn about (eventually) after their sweet little babies have all grown up and struck out for lives of their own. In the most basic definition, a sibling is pretty much the first best friend that any person could ever ask for. Even if they do something to make you mad or say something to otherwise irritate you, siblings are *always* there when you need them. While it's been said that brothers tend to be very protective of their sisters, the same holds true the other way, too. "Nobody but sisters have the right to annoy their brothers!"

Brandon had two older siblings in his life right from the start though over the years as life unfolded, he gained additional stepfamily as well. Brandon's older sister Nicole was a part of his life from day one.

"Some of the earliest memories I have of Brandon go back to when he was just a toddler. I remember playing 'Dress Up' with him, dressing him up like I did my baby dolls. I also remember playing 'Barber Shop' with him too, and cutting off all his hair. Of course, being the middle child (and the *only* girl) I'd get both Brandon and our older brother Chris to play Barbie's with me, too."

"Brandon was a loyal person. He was many things: funny, dependable, honest, loving, the list is long. To choose only one quality about my brother is difficult because he possessed so many great ones. If I had to elaborate though, it'd have to be about his tremendous sense of humor. When Brandon would get tickled about something, he'd let out this great belly laugh and you just couldn't help but laugh right along with him. His laughter was contagious. Brandon was constantly telling jokes and pranking people. He was so damn funny, always working to get a good laugh out of anyone. He had a way of making light of situations with his humor and could make you feel better about whatever was bringing you down in an instant. I miss that so much, him and his jokes. I can still hear his laughter in my head. I hope it never fades away."

"About stories I might like to share about my brother, there are lots I could tell, including some I'm sure Brandon wouldn't want me to share. We were always into mischief growing up, always playing pranks on people. I laugh every time I tell this story but I remember one time when we were kids, Mom and I were sitting out in the living room just talking when all of a sudden we heard these loud popping noises coming from Brandon's room. Mom and I knew it couldn't be good, so we ran to open the door."

"Mom opened the door but immediately had to close it. There was Brandon, scared shitless, hiding under his bunk-bed with his hands over the top of his head and his entire room filled with smoke. He'd decided to set off a bag of bottle rockets and every single one of them went off! Mom slammed the door closed and had to wait until the last rocket went off before going back in. I laughed until I cried. The entire back of the house was filled with smoke. We were all coughing and poor Brandon was an absolute mess as he crawled out from under that bed. He knew his ass was grass for lighting up fireworks in his room. I'll never forget that day. The sound of those bottle rockets going off seemed like it'd never end."

"Another thing about Brandon was how that boy loved to eat and cook. One of his favorite dishes was biscuits and gravy. When Brandon cooked, he would take whatever he could find in the cupboard, put a little bit of this and a little bit of that in it and could whip up something that tasted pretty darn good."

"When we were kids, there was some major sibling rivalry between Brandon and me but as we grew older, we became more like two peas in a pod. We always had each other's backs. There's so much that I miss about him: the nights we'd go out and grab a few beers, the times we'd spend cutting up with one another and singing classic rock songs at the top of our lungs, and of course I have to mention those big bonfires he'd set up…"

"Our brothers and sisters are there with us from the dawn of our personal stories to the inevitable dusk."
— S.S. Merrell

"When I first found out about what had happened with Brandon, I was living in San Diego. We've always been a close-knit family, but at that particular time in our lives, we were all living in different states. I remember Mom called the house early that morning, asking for my husband (TJ). I knew something was terribly wrong just by the sound of her voice but nothing could have prepared me for what she had to say. The moment I heard her convey that my brother had taken his own life, it felt as if all the air had instantly been sucked out of the room. I remember this burning sensation running through my body as I screamed and cried out in disbelief. I could not/did not want to believe it."

"It's still hard for me. I have a difficult time accepting his death, even today. To cope, I try imagining that he's just gone away on deployment. The Brandon I knew would never do something like take his own life. It pains me to think that maybe I could have saved him or done something to change the outcome. I'll never understand suicide. Losing Brandon has left us all with gaping holes in our hearts that can never be filled."

In putting Brandon's story to paper, there was opportunity to ask prior service members about their personal experience with the transitional process. Transition is that period immediately after active duty where military persons have completed their terms of enlistment and return to non-military status i.e. civilians. Brandon's sister Nicole is a Veteran of the United States Air Force.

"Transition out of the Air Force for me was pretty seamless. My husband (a Marine) and I were both stationed in Hawaii at the time but I chose to leave the military early because we were expecting our first child. I wanted to be sure I'd be home with our new baby instead of facing possible deployment away from him for any time. It was the best decision I could have ever made. As I've said, my husband was in the Marines and ended up deploying three weeks after our oldest was born. It wasn't easy being a new mom all by myself living clear across the country from the rest of my family."

"I remember the first time Brandon ever met his oldest nephew. I was living in Hawaii at the time and my husband TJ was on deployment. Brandon's unit was just coming back from its deployment and his detachment had docked in Pearl Harbor for the day. I picked him and his buddy up and drove them back to base. They only had a few hours before they had to be back on the ship so they showered and grabbed something to eat before we all jumped back into my car. I wanted to take them on a little site-seeing tour and show them as much of the island as I could during the few hours they had before they had to be back."

"More has to be done to stop Veteran suicide. It's completely heart-breaking how so many individuals feel that's the only way to stop the war going on inside their heads. Twenty-two (plus one) Veterans a day is shocking! It's an astronomical number and completely unacceptable: even one is too many! I feel there should be more policies and procedures set into place *before* they leave to help protect our Veterans returning from deployment. Mental health is vital. The civilian population should be more aware and better educated regarding the signs and symptoms of PTSD."

4 -TAYLOR 'TJ' HARRIS-

"When a vet is left alone with his voices, you don't always know who's going to be stronger."

Mr. Taylor (TJ) Harris is a Veteran of the United States Marine Corps with five deployments to his credit. It's been told that if anybody were to look for that one person who had the biggest influence on Brandon Ladner and his determining to become a Marine himself, it would be *this* man, his brother-in-law TJ Harris.

"One of the earliest memories I have of Brandon took place one weekend when I was still stationed in South Carolina. I was dating his sister Nicole and had returned to Alabama with a friend of mine. Whenever I'd go to Alabama, I'd always visit with Nicole and the family. This one particular weekend, Brandon had hinted he needed a haircut. Now, you know Marines and haircuts; that's our area of expertise. (We all had to get one on a weekly basis.) My buddy Calen and I jumped at the opportunity to give this young, motivated individual (Brandon) a nice high & tight (haircut) just like we had. Unfortunately, his cut didn't turn out as well as any of us had expected."

"Calen and I ended up dying laughing at the result. Brandon was a good sport about it, but I know he was pissed. We tried to quit laughing but just couldn't stop, even though we probably should have. It wasn't all that long ago I saw pictures of Calen and I doing that, cutting Brandon's hair at his mom's. That was a fun memory."

"Brandon and I weren't as close as I'd have liked to have been because I was in the Corps and seemed to continuously be away on deployment. But he was always confident, tremendously funny and such a nice guy. Brandon was a great kid who truly loved his family and all of his friends."

"There was another time, Brandon and I ended up at a nearby lake by his mom's house. I grew up just a few blocks away but never knew the place existed. Brandon had found a canoe in the middle of nowhere with only one paddle. We ended up sitting out there in the middle of that lake just sharing a lot of words about life, the Corps and whatnot. He was just like his sister, too and always wanted to play the "What If?" game. (What if I was rich? What if I was a doctor?) That night we were out there at the lake, Brandon came up with some good 'What ifs?'"

"Everything started for me around the time I was transitioning out of the Marines. Nothing bothered me while I was still in the Corps; I actually had a successful transition process but am currently dealing with my own PTSD. My memory seems to have gotten worse as time has passed. I remember one day talking in the car with Nicole, discussing news she'd heard on the radio about some car wreck and how one person had died at the scene. I expressed to her how crazy it would be to experience coming up on an accident like that. She responded, '*You did, when you were on recruiting duty.*' It took me a while to remember it."

"I made my disability claim in San Diego and then took my exams at the VA in Birmingham. I have no complaints; some suggestions maybe, but no complaints. I did all I was asked to do in a timely manner and got the results back for my disability claim within six months. The Lord has blessed me my entire life."

"I saw Brandon as a man who worked hard for what he wanted and would do anything to make it happen. When Nicole told me about his death, I felt for her, the whole family. Back when Nicole and I were just starting to date, I'd lost my seventeen-year-old brother Josh to a car crash. Having lost a sibling myself, my heart automatically dropped. I knew what was coming and how she would feel. Until recently, I couldn't see how PTSD could so provoke anybody to commit suicide, but when a vet is left alone with his voices, you don't always know who's going to be stronger."

-To the Beginning of Better Understanding-

TM Fitzgerald

5 -SEMPER FI: ALWAYS FAITHFUL-
"Those words are a battle cry, a greeting and a legend in the Marine Corps."

In an article entitled *Marine Looks Back on Beirut Bombing* originally published in the New York Times, December 02, 1986 the significant impact, emotion and feelings behind the Latin phrase '*Semper Fidelis*' was exemplified by the humble actions of one survivor (and Marine) named Jeffrey Nashton. It was with great difficulty that Nashton conveyed those two seemingly unassuming words to a four-star general with whom he was communicating with in the beginning stages of his recovery after the terrorist bombing of the Marine Barracks in Lebanon in October of 1983.

From the same article, former President Ronald Reagan shared the following: *"If you've been a Marine or if, like myself, you're an admirer of the Marines, then you know those words are a battle cry, a greeting and a legend in the Marine Corps. They're Marine shorthand for the motto of the Corps - Semper Fidelis - 'always faithful.' "*

One hundred years before the fatal October 23, 1983, terroristic bombing of the Marine barracks in Lebanon, Beirut, the United States Marines officially adopted and gave the world *Semper Fidelis: Always Faithful.* This maxim *"guides Marines to remain faithful to the mission at hand, to each other, to the Corps and country, no matter what."*

Brandon Ladner certainly paid his dues. After earning his eagle, globe, and anchor, he adapted '*Semper Fi*' as a personal way of life. From all outward appearances, Ladner was never the guy whom anyone pictured determined to take his own life. On September 09, 2014, after losing his personal battle with the demon that is PTSD, Marine Sgt. Brandon Charles Ladner joined an alarming number of Veterans and took his life here at home. (Incidentally, Ladner was not the first and sadly enough, not the last Marine from his unit who felt so compelled.)

> *"The deadliest battlefields aren't remote deserts or faraway countries but our own living rooms, bedrooms, backyards, and garages. These battlefields are unexpected. That makes you stop and think…"*
>
> -Daniel Pradilla

Before a country actively steps into the theater of war, there is an unspoken yet conscious awareness and knowledge of death. It's a real possibility, almost a given. Every single day, while the good people 'back home' woke and readied for work, debating if they had time to stop off for a quick coffee on their way to the office, half a world away were young men stepping off into their mornings playing the *'I wonder if…'* game. Every day that they fought, they wondered; *'I wonder if today is the day I will die?'*

"Tomorrow is never guaranteed." Nowhere is that fact more glaringly obvious than for those positioned in the theater of active war/conflict. Actually, it doesn't matter which side you're on or what place you hold in the fight: death is a potential somewhere for someone, a constant consideration for all. Statistically, if by nothing else than the virtue of it being war, somebody is going to die. It's going to happen to someone, *somewhere*, at some point in time. One side will win, the other will lose.

Civilians have been purposefully insulated from the military. All the good people 'back home' are quite content with struggling with their daily coffee decision. It demonstrates how Americans and their military have drifted apart. *"For nearly two generations, no American has been obligated to join the military and few do."* People rarely make room for civic obligations in today's world, so when casualties occur during times of war, essentially the best that anyone can hope for from the people back home is that maybe they'll acknowledge the news shared via various media outlets about the fallen. In reality, most people will maybe shake their heads and shrug their shoulders as names of the fallen slowly stream home from the battlefields. *'Did you read about that Johnson boy?'* *'We lost another one'* as they wait in line for their Frappuccino. That's about as close as they'll ever get to their inner patriot or connect to war.

For the vast majority of Americans, war is something that only happens in other countries, at least in their minds and if something unfortunate happens to somebody they don't know?

In 2011, Sabrina Tavernise wrote, *"Conflicts and the people who fight them are not part of most people's everyday lives."* We, as a society as a whole, are paying the price for this disconnect because what is happening to so many of our Veterans after they return from conflict is of no interest to the public at large. Society has narrowed the view, downplaying the magnitude of mortality suffered by its own Freedom Forces, but in doing so, we began playing with fire.

At the height of war, stories of uninvited, unwelcome knocks on unsuspecting doors where parents, spouses or other loved ones were greeted by groups of casualty affairs officers became the norm instead of the exception. People opened doors across this nation thousands of times and knew instantly somebody wasn't coming home. Casualty Affairs became a routine occurrence all across America. It seemed in many people's minds, death owing to war only happened 'over there.' In the United States of America, nobody *ever* expected to hear about the loss of life on the home front. People essentially desensitized themselves from the possibility. That just wasn't how war worked in their minds. Unfortunately, they couldn't have been more wrong.

It's been written in recent years that the effects of this country's latest wars have been particularly stressful for, among a few other reasons, the fact that 'front lines' were never clearly defined. War was happening *everywhere*, all around, a statement that rang true on several levels. War wasn't something to 'get away' from. Even after the official 'the war is over' decree, another war began long after troops left their posts in the battlefields. Nobody adequately warned them, and so many were hesitant to acknowledge it once it became apparent. It was a lesson that should have been learned in other battles, other wars long ago. Apparently, nobody thought to develop official 'rules of engagement' for preventing soldier suicide.

We *all* have personal demons to contend with. Of course, some of us carry around more than others, doing battle with them every day. This fact can be debilitating for Veterans in particular, and in attempting to deal with those things has caused many to avoid seeking out the help so many desperately need. Countless individuals choose to self-medicate, over-medicate and at the harshest extreme, take their own life. Many who have been to war return with/develop PTSD a demon that carries with it a tremendous and unwelcome stigma.

For those who have never 'been there,' they can't understand why there is such hesitancy for those affected by it to mention the nightmares, report the depression or feelings of guilt so often associated with its evolution. We've made it that way and those on the outside looking in appear to have little to no empathy. *"They volunteered. They knew what they were potentially getting themselves into."* (Remember that little word 'empathy?')

Noel Guerrero once interviewed, *"War leaves you with a dark shadow you can never take away."* Current statistics pertaining to the number of Veterans taking their own lives each day speaks volumes to that fact. The numbers most often quoted when talking about PTSD-related suicides is a debatable, ever-changing, challenged, and sometimes refuted one. *'It's a fallacy.' 'It's not accurate.' 'That can't be right.'* Pick your favorite argument. Any way you look at it, it's a sad development, a truth that nobody wants to acknowledge.

Retired Army general (and West Point grad) Ray Odierno stated the following:

> *"Every soldier (or in this case, Marine) is important, and when we lose a soldier/Marine, it's a big deal, regardless of whether it's through suicide, a motorcycle accident, or combat. Suicides are particularly concerning though because that means that something was happening in that soldiers/Marines life that was so bad, he believed that the only way out was to take his own life. It is incumbent on us to prevent things from getting to that point."*

6 -INTO THE FIRE-
"You can't know unless you've been there."

Life is a personal journey that gives each of us a very unique story to tell. In making our way through this thing called life, each of us earns our own marks of merit. The good stories will ideally generate or evoke deep emotions: maybe a little compassion, some curiosity, or perhaps even a certain degree of satisfaction (depending on the subject matter and audience, of course.) What about the bad ones? Well, that all depends.

For many, their journey through life has been multifaceted. Take Veterans for instance. There is one particular branch of the military where *every* recruit's rite of passage begins within a fearful standing of a pair of yellow footprints. (For people who've never stood in said footprints, that detail alone should naturally generate some level of curiosity.) In select individuals, the mere mention of said footprints is enough to evoke powerful memories and emotion, particularly when you think about what those select few have accomplished after stepping out of those footprints: overcoming all the mystery and initial fear, and gaining the eventual satisfaction of becoming a United States Marine. What motivates one to become a Marine?

Every Marine (and all other Veteran of the United States military, for that matter) has taken the same oath to 'defend this country against all enemies foreign and domestic.' *Every* Marine who has attained the title once stood on a set of those yellow footprints at one time or another. So yes, to a certain degree, repetition of certain facts and details can and *should* be expected when reading stories written about any United States Marine, but what about that number 'twenty-two'? Bad enough, that unacceptable statistic was holding fast at eighteen when the seeds for this project were first sown. Brandon Ladner's story sprang into existence because of the sad repetition of that particular number: twenty-two, a scary, repeating figure that few outside the military realm appear knowledgeable about. Repetition to this extent was never expected.

Unless you're prior military, (or as in Brandon's example, a Marine), the various combinations of numbers, letters, unit names and company designations used in this book will likely mean nothing to you. (It's all about organization, by the way.) So while the fact may be that this book is about one Marine specifically, it was written to share with the rest of the world: to share, to educate and teach.

"You can't know unless you've been there." While these seven words are an undeniable military truth, (particularly among combat Veterans) that phrase also rings true in respect to events in every other life, paralleling another oft-heard phrase: "Walk a mile in my shoes before you dare to judge." So it goes with the 1/5 (and every other battalion: Marine or otherwise.)

Sharing facts from a popular web-based data site, the 1st Battalion, 5th Marines (commonly referred to as simply the 1/5) is a United States Marine infantry battalion based out of Camp Pendleton, California and consists of both Marines and sailors. The 1/5 falls under the command of the 5th Marine Regiment, 1st Marine Division and was first formed in 1914 and has served in every major conflict the United States has been involved in since.

The 1/5 was initially formed July 13, 1914. Despite the battalion being disbanded by Christmas Eve that same year, it was reactivated by May 1917. The 1/5 deployed to France that June and fought in numerous campaigns. It is one of just two regiments authorized to wear the French Fourragère. Members of the 5th and 6th Marine Regiments wear the Fourragère to represent multiple awarding of the 'Croix de Guerre,' a military accolade bestowed upon the Marines by the French government in World War I.

The 1/5 made its most prominent impact in Belleau Wood, Germany in June of 1918. Over three hundred Marines lost their lives here and additionally, Gunnery Sergeant Ernest A. Janson became the first Marine to earn the Medal of Honor in World War I. By August of 1919, the 1/5 was once again deactivated and would not be reactivated again until fifteen years later.

In November 1934, the 1st Battalion was reactivated only to be deactivated four short months later. By April of 1940, 1st Battalion was again reactivated and fighting in the Pacific campaigns of Guadalcanal, New Guinea, Peleliu, and Okinawa. In April 1946, their mission accomplished, 1st Battalion was disbanded, and most Veterans returned to civilian life. During October 1949, it was reactivated and by the following August, deployed to the Republic of Korea. Names such as the Pusan Perimeter, Inchon, Seoul and Chosin Reservoir were added to the Battalion's battle vocabulary. At the close of hostilities, the 1/5 returned to the United States, settling at Camp Pendleton."

From June 1966 to March 1971, the 1/5 deployed to Vietnam, playing a major role in the Battle of Hue City during February 1968. Engaging the enemy in the famous Citadel on the north side of the Perfume River, the 1/5 became known as the 'Citadel Battalion.' The unit was again deactivated in June 1974 but quickly reactivated nine months later.

The 1/5 was part of the Persian Gulf War as well as Operations Desert Shield and Storm. "They deployed to Kuwait in 2003 to become part of the invasion force that ousted Saddam Hussein. The Marines of 1/5 were the first to enter the country starting combat operations the day prior to the beginning of the war..." The battle for Baghdad followed and then they returned to Al Anbar Province, Iraq for Operation Iraqi Freedom (OIF). After combat operations in Helmand, the 1/5 was once more deployed to Afghanistan to support Operation Enduring Freedom (OEF).

Camaraderie and fellowship of the United States Marine Corps are as legendary as the yellow footprints at Marine Corps Recruit Depot (MCRD). Across generations, there are facts about the Corps that still apply to this day. 'You don't join the Marines. You become one.' 'The title is earned, never given.' None of that stops just because an individual completes his/her term of enlistment

(EAS). It's not the way his own story panned out, but by choosing to become a Marine, Brandon Ladner was prepared to fight and even die for his country.

'*Duty, honor, country-,*' Although speaking to cadets at his Alma Mater West Point, in his May 12, 1969, speech, five-star General of the Army Douglas MacArthur spoke suitably descriptive words that bore relevance to one particular Marine who wasn't even due to enter the world for eighteen more years.

> "*Duty. Honor. Country. The code which those words perpetuate embraces the highest moral laws and will stand the test of any ethics or philosophies ever promulgated for the uplift of mankind. Its requirements are for the things that are right, and its restraints are from the things that are wrong. The soldier (or in this case, a Marine named Brandon Ladner) above all other men, is required to practice the greatest act of training - sacrifice. In battle and in the face of danger and death, he discloses divine attributes which the Maker gave when he created man in his own image. No physical courage and no brute instinct can take the place of the Divine help which alone can sustain him. However horrible the incidents of war may be, the soldier who is called upon to offer and to give his life for his country, is the noblest development of mankind.*"

It wasn't on the battlefield, but Brandon Ladner still gave his life for this country.

7 -BIVOUAC OF THE DEAD-

(Bivouac of the dead is a poem written by Danville, Kentucky native, Theodore O'Hara to honor his fellow soldiers from Kentucky who died in the Mexican-American war 1846-1848.)

> *The muffled drum's sad roll has beat*
> *The soldier's last tattoo;*
> *No more on life's parade shall meet*
> *That brave and fallen few.*
> *On Fame's eternal camping-ground*
> *Their silent tents are spread,*
> *And Glory guards, with solemn round,*
> *The bivouac of the dead...*

Tragedy is a word defining great loss or misfortune. What makes something tragic? Devastating? Appalling? Disturbing? Earth-shattering? It's a very particular word, tragedy and there is no clearly defined, universally accepted definition that applies to *every* situation declared as such.

An undeniable sign of the times is the fact that thousands of young American soldiers and Marines have perished while serving 'in-country' during modern war. However, a fact that's only been recently publicized reveals how now, more Veterans have taken their own lives *after* returning home than the number of those who have died in-country. In other words, the number of service members who have taken their own lives has surpassed the number killed in combat. Tragic? *"Absolutely,"* Former Marine Staff Sergeant Nickomar Santana responded. Summing that unfortunate data with the following, Santana followed up his brief comment: *"-it's the responsibility of those of us left behind to remember them all."*

The intent was never to focus *From Motorcycles to Machine Guns* on the heartbreaking event that marked the conclusion of Brandon Ladner's life; instead, this biographical sketch was born from a promise to help raise awareness of a condition affecting so many of America's defenders. However, in sharing Brandon's life, his story had to be told in its entirety.

Those who knew and lived by him already know the sad details of his passing and in theory; it should be enough for the rest of the world simply to know Brandon Ladner *"became one of the twenty-two."* However, the majority of the population have no idea what that number means. In writing and sharing his story, one very important fact that must be made clear; Brandon Ladner did not become just another number, rather, what happened to this man made his necessary story to share.

George Washington once said, "*The willingness with which our young people are likely to serve in any war, no matter how justified, shall be directly proportional to how they perceive the Veterans of earlier wars were treated and appreciated by the nation.*"

The *Huffington Post* shared how America professes to hold its military members and Veterans in high esteem, honoring them for their service. This respect for the military -- as well as providing service members with benefits for housing, food, and health care -- is *essential* to maintaining moral as well as ensuring a continuing stream of qualified recruits into the all-volunteer force. This isn't the reality. Ask *any* Viet Nam Veteran, Enewetak Veteran, ask any Veteran at all about respect and esteem. Ask any of them how the government it fought for lends a blind eye to its own.

PTSD is a real threat challenging our military men and women. Suicide rates among all service members (which, by the way (at least at the time of this books' creation had reached a thirty-year high) have become a significant public health crisis that must be better addressed than the way things are going today. While military service has historically been protective against reporting suicide among active duty personnel, the dramatic rise in the suicide rate since 2005 among this particular population group indicates this is no longer the case. □

In sharing the story of Brandon Ladner, there also came an obligation to educate. The intent was to go beyond the obligatory, '*Gee, that's too bad*' sort of comments and drive the point home. It's not simply 'somebody else's' problem, or 'only a Marine problem.' PTSD is *everybody's* problem and goes far beyond challenging people to twenty-two push-ups a day or wearing t-shirts with flashy graphics. The following material is shared from the website of the esteemed Mayo Clinic in Rochester, Minnesota.

The proceeding information appears twice in this book and has been shared in such a fashion quite on purpose; **one set of pages is to leave intact in this book and the other has been provided to pull out and share. Read it. Study it. Post it. Spread the word. Educate yourself.** Make, 'I didn't know' and 'I never saw it coming' obsolete phrases. Empower yourself and reach out to those who are broken. Help bring them back. Let them know that asking for help is not a sign of weakness.

> "*We call one another survivors but don't often take the time to think about what that really means. What it means, is that people are still here. What it means, is that you faced down something that no one should ever have to and that even this terrible thing was not enough to stop you. What it means, is that you are incredibly strong, even in the moments when you yourself don't know that.*"

□

8 -BROKEN ARROWS DON'T FLY STRAIGHT-
Signs and Symptoms of PTSD: A Page to Share
Post-traumatic stress disorder (PTSD)
(A second set to tear out appears at end of this book.)

Post-traumatic stress disorder (PTSD) is a mental health condition triggered by experiencing or witnessing a terrifying event: ANY event. It could be war, rape, a near-death experience, ANY *traumatic* event. Symptoms may include (but are not limited to) flashbacks, nightmares, and severe anxiety, as well as uncontrollable thoughts about the event. PTSD can be experienced by *anyone*: man, woman, child, civilian, military, etc. PTSD does *not* discriminate.

Many who have experienced traumatic events have difficulty adjusting and coping for a while, but with time and good self-care, they usually get better. If the symptoms get worse or last for months or even years and interfere with daily functioning, then it may be PTSD. Post-traumatic stress disorder symptoms may start within three months of a traumatic event, but sometimes symptoms (which can cause significant problems in social or work situations and in relationships) may not appear until years following. Symptoms may include:

* Recurrent, unwanted distressing memories of traumatic event
* Reliving the event as if it were happening again (flashbacks)
* Upsetting dreams
* Severe emotional distress/physical reactions to things reminding person of the event
* Negative feelings
* Inability to experience positive emotions
* Feeling emotionally numb
* Lack of interest in once enjoyable activities

- Hopelessness about the future
- Memory problems, including not remembering important aspects of the traumatic event
- Difficulty maintaining close relationships
- Changes in emotional reactions
- Irritability, angry outbursts or aggressive behavior
- Always on guard for danger
- Overwhelming guilt or shame
- Self-destructive behavior, such as drinking too much or driving too fast
- Trouble concentrating
- Trouble sleeping
- Being easily startled or frightened
- Intensity of symptoms

PTSD symptoms can vary in intensity over time and individuals may have more symptoms when he or she is stressed in general, or when they run into reminders of what they went through. For example, a Veteran may hear a car backfire and relive some traumatic combat experience, or a woman may see a report on the news about a sexual assault and feel overcome by memories of her own assault.

If a person has disturbing thoughts and feelings about a traumatic event for more than a month, if they're severe, or if that person is having trouble getting his/her life back under control, encourage them to talk to a health care professional and get treatment as soon as possible to help prevent PTSD symptoms from getting worse.

If you or someone you know is having suicidal thoughts, get help right away.

- Reach out to a close friend or loved one.
- Call a suicide hotline number — in the United States, call the National Suicide Prevention Lifeline at 800-273-TALK (800-273-8255) to reach a trained counselor. Use that same number and press 1 to reach the Veterans Crisis Line.

If you know someone in danger of committing suicide or has made a suicide attempt, make sure someone stays with that person. Call 911 or the local emergency number immediately or take the person to the nearest hospital emergency room.

The following pages have previously appeared in the book *Ghosts in the Gray* and are shared here by permission.

9 -DÉJÀVU-

"A nation is defined by its heroes."
- Peter Collier

"Who kept the faith and fought the fight; the glory theirs, the duty ours."
-Wallace Bruce

"The world breaks everyone and afterward many are strong at the broken places."
- Ernest Hemingway

"But what about the ones who aren't, Mr. Hemingway?"
-TM Fitzgerald

☐ What is post-traumatic stress disorder? (AKA PTS or PTSD.) Think of this condition in the most general and broadest of terms: a serious case of 'same shit, different war.' It needs to be realized that this disorder has been a very specific part of the military identity for generations. That is *not* to say PTSD is occupation, gender, age or *"any other type person, place, or occupation exclusive"* by any means. (It's *not*, but keep in mind the fact that this book is about one specific Marine and how PTSD affected *him* and *his* world.) The intent here is not to refute any statistics or rewrite information already available for people to research. However, if more people had a better understanding of PTSD, maybe more lives could be saved. The wild assortment of facts, statements and quotes shared so far has been meant to educate and be shared.

"War's effects are not always apparent."

-Bica

Collected from the previously published book entitled, *Ghosts in the Gray*, the following information reflects an irreversible resolution carried out by a current average of twenty-two military Veterans each day. PTSD has reared its ugly head too many times, driving many to make the ultimate and sadly desperate decision to end their own life, a resolution affecting the remaining reality of survivors more profoundly than any could ever know.

"What is this PTSD and why should I care?' Perhaps better questions to ask would be, *"Why the hell have we been reporting the fact that twenty-two Veterans a day are committing suicide? Why has this been called a misunderstood statistic? Why should anybody pay attention to this information?"* All of that is about to be explained.

In December of 2013, Alan Zarembo published an article in the Los Angeles Times that shared the following:

> *"In most discussions of suicide and the wars in Iraq and Afghanistan, there's one statistic that gets repeated most: twenty-two Veterans kill themselves each day. That number comes from a study published in early 2013 by researchers at the federal Department of Veterans Affairs. But the recent wars were not the study's primary focus. (In fact, they play a minor role in Veteran suicides overall.)*
>
> *VA researchers used death records from 21 states to come up with a 2010 national estimate for Veterans of all ages. As a group, veterans are old. Military service being far rarer than it was in the days of the draft, more than 91% of the nation's 22 million Veterans are at least 35 years old, and an overwhelming majority did not serve in the post-9/11 era.*
>
> *About 72% of Veterans are at least fifty years old. It's not surprising, then, that the VA found that people in this age group account for 69% of Veteran suicides — or more than fifteen of the twenty-two per day statistic."*

We, as a grateful nation need to acknowledge and help all our Veterans but particularly the ones of *this* generation today. We *all* need to step up, step forward and make sure they don't become statistics of tomorrow. There have been far too many misconceptions about whom or how this process called PTSD affects lives: even from the people this tends to affect the most.

For as long as the condition has existed, it appears little to no tangible strides have been made in treating PTSD other than zealously poly-pharming excessive scripts of barely off the shelf (just past the 'guinea-pig' phase II stage of pharmaceutical research) drugs and doling out unproven 'therapies-of-the-week' to those this has affected most: combat soldiers and Marines. (To reiterate once again, this collaboration is by *no* means saying that these specific Veterans are the *only* people who experience PTSD exclusively or that it's only Veterans, period. However, that's what this book is about and so that is the context this condition is addressed in here.)

True enough, we live in a time where the entire world has become steadily less concerned with its freedom forces. "They knew what they were in for." "They knew the possibilities…" They, they, they. In his book, *Broken Bones, Shattered Minds*, Dr. Ronald J. Glassner appeared to accentuate that fact when he wrote the following:

> *"Over the last forty years, we've become a country that has grown more distant, less involved, and less concerned about its military."*

Before Dr. Glassner, renowned author George Orwell pointed out the following:

> *"People sleep peacefully in their beds at night only because rough men stand ready to do violence on their behalf."*

And last but not least, the following sentiment: (Which can be attributed to an anonymous Veteran of the Afghani war who struggled with the condition personally.) \

> *"We'd be out there in the middle of BFA (AKA 'Bumb-Fuck Afghanistan') where the desert met the sky, searching for 'that place' only we never found 'that place,' you know, like the one everybody searches for at the end of a God-damned rainbow? Whenever we got there, 'that place' always seemed just a little further away. We went, and we fought but what the hell for? Our presence never seemed to go beyond the search for WMD*

45

(weapons of mass destruction) and then ISIS came in and took back everything we had gained. How many of our brothers died for that? How many came home under a flag instead of saluting it? We were supposed to know what we were in for but none of us were supposed to be affected by what happened? By what we did or saw? Who was the brilliant mind behind this determination?"

Nobody knows who to attribute the following information to: *"Don't let the past control you"* but whoever made that declaration must have thought himself positively brilliant. After all, is it not the past that shapes our future? Something each of us is supposed to learn from? Or more to the point, (in some cases) parts of the past are things that some of us would like to change or forget entirely?

To an extent, the past certainly *does* exert at least some degree of control over the rest of our lives, but for many Veterans, that particular maxim is merely a platitude: something much easier for everybody else to say than for an affected Vet to do. For those struggling with PTSD? Hell yes, the past is *certainly* an affecting and controlling portion of present life. There are things that cannot be unseen or undone, things people have to live with for the rest of their lives and some of these are the very things that drive many to the edge with no prospect of turning back.

The platitude too quickly became a tired and overly worn-out phrase assuredly expressed by an inexperienced 'somebody' sitting behind the sanctuary of an antique desk somewhere back in Washington, D.C. Whatever their intent, that person somehow felt compelled, or maybe even pressured to convey meaningful counsel (and maybe it was on some level) to rally the troops and encourage their supporters. However, for many Vets, those six words were merely an over-used, second-hand expression quoted from or stolen off some pre-fabricated, pre-printed treatment plan at the local VA. The words, though well-intended, mean nothing.

The truth of the matter is, with PTSD, people on the outside who've never seriously taken the time to look at a troubled Vet's existence don't know anything is wrong; not at first glance. PTSD starts small. Maybe that vet shuts down and disconnects; he/she quits talking to people like he/she used to or maybe begins appearing more on edge. Maybe there's nothing so noticeable at all. People on the outside likely chalk up circumstances they can't explain as that person just having an off day or 'that guy' not coping well with some problem at home: something comparatively ordinary for anybody else in the scheme of life. PTSD is a demon that likes to introduce itself in the lonely hours, slipping in with the shadows that slide across the floor. Just like how subjective its effects are on the people it ensnares, PTSD cannot be blamed on the action (or lack thereof) of any one particular organization or another.

Friends and family are not prepared for the changes that can follow their military members home after active-duty. (Neither were those Veterans, nor as it turned out, the Veteran's Healthcare Administration AKA 'The VA'.) Many Veterans, who utilize what resources they may be given, seek what help they can and, if they aren't turned away, are essentially told to '*suck it up*' or '*deal with it.*' "*Here take these pills and you'll be fine. We'll see if we can schedule your follow-up visit in six months.*" Unfortunately, there is a stigma in asking for help, one that we need to eradicate. Each branch of service has developed its own suicide prevention program and each branch does its own post-deployment health screenings and debriefings but what has happened to so many of this country's warriors that made them so prepared, so prone to carrying out one final mission?

The Marine persona in particular projects a distinct sense of invincibility. "*First to fight!*" "*Be strong!*" "*Don't be that guy!*" "*You've got this!*" This is not to imply that it's only Marines who compile the current statistic but unfortunately, that figure has turned into something all too typical; no longer a rarity (was it ever?) The "*I didn't know*" factor long gone, nobody has wanted to talk about it. (Conveniently enough, nobody seems to have noticed how long it took for that statistic (currently twenty-two a day) to be recognized in the first place.) Twenty-two is one hell of a revelation regarding the pervading number of Veterans who have died by their *own* hand *after* coming home from deployment overseas.

> "*These guys could face the enemy, but when they came home, they couldn't face their problems. It became their norm. Nobody felt like they were messed up because they all felt that way at first. They convinced themselves there wasn't any problem and they carried on, but then, they came home...*"
>
> -Santana

For a story to have any impact, it cannot be told from just one, solitary angle. It must be told from and directed to the most significant angle: *theirs*. However, for many, that angle no longer exists. *"Who's going to tell their story now?"* How can anybody tell those Veterans' tales when the stories people have already convinced themselves begin with; *"Things couldn't possibly have been that bad. He'd never have let it go that far." "Leave him alone. Let him work through it by himself. He'll ask for help if he wants it."* Too many of those stories have sadly turned into, *"Does anybody know what's going on with (insert Veteran name here.)?" "We lost another one"* or *"Never figured him to be the one to have any problems."* So far, it appears that the only thing the current administration deems necessary to accomplish is to run more government-funded studies or otherwise examine why 'the system' (AKA the 'VA') continues in failing our Veterans. They don't need any more studies. The VA alone is not solely to blame. They, *our* Veterans need *our* help.

There's been plenty of informative material written and posted about post-traumatic stress to be sure, but most of it has been clinical and gray as opposed to solid black and white. Many books and periodicals have delved into great detail describing the development of what has most currently been labeled post-traumatic stress disorder, or more commonly PTSD. (Remember? *Same shit, different war?'* PTSD is not anything new.) It's a condition that has worked its way through previous generations under a variety of different terms. (*"A rose by any other name…"*)

Many people will simply choose to sit back, maybe scratch their head a bit or shrug their shoulders and quickly forget they ever read anything about this affliction. Others may think there should have been more information presented by way of facts, figures or other statistics. There's already enough of that available to the public, to our Veterans yet the numbers are still there, still fluctuating.

The Veterans Administration has published statistics, private research firms have compiled studies, and various arguments and debates have been brought to the table. PTSD is *real*, not a figment of the imagination. It is a condition that needs to be addressed and discussed in the context it's being addressed here. No matter the war, no matter the generation, PTSD seems to be that pig in lipstick that continues being swept under the carpet. The point being is that no matter how much you apply, a pig in lipstick is *still* a pig. PTSD is not going to magically disappear.

One literary resource described PTSD with various clinical details inclusive of listing some of the more commonly prescribed medications and therapies currently being used to treat it. That same publication also contained page upon page of nonspecific information regarding how the disorder has been addressed and 'treated' in the past. That book contained *nothing* particularly revealing aside from the list of medications. What about the PTSD process itself? Why all the tap-dancing on eggshells? Information, please.

Another resource began its rather generic recount of PTSD by discussing other cultures and their associated religions. There was *nothing* about advances in screenings, treatments or medicine: nothing but dozens of pages to wade through before PTSD was so much as even addressed as it pertained to the American military condition. What did PTSD have to do with prevailing religions in Ghana or with sheep herders in the Swiss Alps? It was easy to see how the average person reading that stuff could end up shaking their head and throwing the book across the table. They'd never find the exact information they set out searching for in the first place.

> *"It's no wonder the people affected by this phenomenon have such a difficult time with it. Everybody who has bothered to address the issue has danced around it without a clue, researching and studying but so far unable to effectively do anything about it."*

One of the last clinical publications used as a reference wound up taking the almost predictable 'one size fits all' approach. It revealed how many people mistakenly believe PTSD is a 'men's only' issue or only affects combat Veterans. Post-traumatic stress disorder is *not* specific to just the military or *only* men. *Any* traumatic event can elicit what is often diagnosed as PTSD in any walk of life: this includes men, women, and children. Victims of violent crime, sexual abuse, people who've had near-death experiences and even those individuals who've survived catastrophic events, (weather calamities, war) etc. can *all* start the dizzying tumble into the realm of PTSD. (Post trauma, meaning anybody who's experienced *any* kind of traumatic event: *anybody*.)

To be fair, there are of course many existing publications available that do a thorough job of explaining the aforementioned and discuss in great detail the need for funding more studies, the necessity of developing new drug therapies, etc. but offer NOTHING new specifically about taking care of returning Veterans. How could anybody with good conscious say PTSD is not real or that they didn't know this was going to happen? History has repeated itself; over and over, yet what have we learned? How are we going to address this after the *next* war experience?

By all outward appearances, it looks as if very few on the psychological side of the house have paid any attention to the fact that we've been (and are still) fighting a different kind of war. These days, the enemy isn't always visible and the injuries inflicted on our troops are often more than what anybody can see. Injuries suffered by our warriors today are moral as well, which compounds the whole PTSD issue.

In 2007, Camillo Bica published an op-ed series. He argued the following point:

> "… *as soldiers experience the horror and cruelty of war, especially guerrilla/counter insurgency war such as was the case in Vietnam and now in Iraq, the moral gravity of their actions – displacing, torturing, injuring, and killing other human beings – becomes apparent and problematic. As a consequence, soldiers suffer not only the effects of trauma, but from debilitating remorse, guilt, shame, disorientation, and alienation from the remainder of the moral community – moral injuries.*"

What do ethics/morality and honor have to do with war? War is war, right? Who cares if anybody's feelings get hurt or if you feel bad about shooting the enemy? He who has the biggest guns wins, right? Get in, get it done and get out! What does decency or fairness have to do with forces engaged in battle, or 'Rules of Engagement' period?

> *"I (Bica) have concluded that the psychological, emotional, and moral injuries of war cannot be cured, that war*

never "goes away." That for far too many, such war injuries are and have been terminal. For others, they are chronic, demanding that Veterans struggle each day through anger, perhaps even rage, guilt, shame, remorse, grave despair, and depression to come to grips with the experience, with "what I have done and what I have become." With luck, and with love and support, the best that can be achieved, is a benign acceptance, understanding, forgiveness, and reconciliation."

We've sent troops to fight in wars where the moral injuries have been just as prevalent as the visible, physical ones. It's because of this fact that long after they come home, we can call these vets 'Victims of Innovation'. (Progress: it happens in war, too.) The battlefield changed, but somebody forgot to tell all the war-ignorant docs and headshrinkers back home about the demons our Veterans were going to be bringing back. (This goes for *all* wars and conflicts since this affliction was first acknowledged and identified: Civil War forward. Have we not learned anything from the past?)

Despite the fact that PTSD has been present in the realm of battle for centuries, the approach to acknowledging and treating it appears to have gone something like this; *"We can't figure out how to effectively 'fix' this so let's just reclassify it, change the name (again) and forget about it until the next war."* PTSD: the (not so) new post-combat norm.

The actual facts of war prove difficult for shrinks and therapists (not to mention the average armchair quarterbacks at home) to understand. As Americans, ours is not a culture of war. So when thousands of men follow the orders of their commander-in-chief and engage in battles on foreign shores, die on foreign shores, war and its after-effects remain a foreign concept to the masses watching from behind. "Nothing like that could ever happen here." (Keep telling yourselves that.)

A person studying the situation might assume that since troops deployed in battles overseas have been a relatively *current* topic in the news and part of our country's history (as opposed to being obscure events taking place 'somewhere else' in history beyond the scope of imagination of people in this generation) that more people are in tune with what's going on with our Veterans when they return home. They're not.

Troops continue being considered collateral damage,

overlooked, taken for granted pawns of wars that nobody has definitively won, wars that many people wonder why we became involved with in the first place. The latest 'Day of Reckoning' already fell upon us long ago. One could easily assume such observations have been made because nobody can yet describe this affliction completely enough to encompass every single person, every case of combat-induced PTSD. Nobody wants to admit that they don't have any answers. The Medical community cannot take a 'one-size fits all' approach, but unfortunately, because of the sheer number of cases, that is *exactly* what it has deemed to do with PTSD.

The final resource publication did a thorough job in describing the positive and negative effects of medications like Zoloft and Trazodone, Paxil and Ambien. It defined the diverse forms of newer antidepressants and various (obscure) psychiatric meds as well as discussing SSRI's (Celexa), antipsychotics, sedatives, and antidepressants. Those medications each may help a person feel less depressed, anxious, or 'on edge,' but they don't treat the *root* causes of PTSD. All the information anyone could ever want about the pharmaceuticals currently prescribed to treat PTSD was there but not a whole lot about how to treat or fix the process itself. (Because of the subjective nature of PTSD, nobody should realistically expect such information any time soon, either.)

For a medical diagnosis or state of disease to be confirmed about a person, there has to be a measurable abnormality in the first place. (Seems like one of those 'no-brainers: "*If you can't identify what's wrong, you can't fix it.*") So when troops come home from combat and figure out that something isn't right, our Veterans try to find help, attempt to figure out and fix what's wrong. All the good doctors and psychiatrists will order the standard battery of tests and screenings and our vets will go through the motions: do what they're told, go to the VA to complete more testing and counseling, but quite often what happens is that the CT scans and MRI's all come back normal. The good physicians and psychiatrists don't see anything wrong. For them, there's nothing tangible to treat. (Evolution, people! It's time to think OUTSIDE the box of conventional medicine. It's time for *serious* change.)

With all the evolution of war tactics and strategies, it seems related thought processes regarding what to do *after* TBI or IEDs have failed to evolve to keep up with the times. The school of thought purported by non-combat experienced doctors who trained in the comfort of expensive medical schools (usually on their parents' dime) comes from studying dated medical periodicals, specialized journals or by reading about other doctors who have studied combat medical issues from afar. What could they know if they never served?

It can't be stressed enough. Post-traumatic stress disorder is *not* unique to any one particular walk of life. Perhaps this condition being such a singular and subjective experience is what has made it so difficult to treat. (There's no money to be made with that revelation though, is there? Dope 'em up, ship 'em out and wash our hands on the whole game.) Are there are no detailed psychological profiles pulled or pre-testing done before anybody goes to war? Not unless their military occupational specialty requires it, so there are no norms to compare medical records with *after* Veterans return home. Depending on the tasks performed by certain Veterans, there may be no records to be found, period. The only progress it seems we've made in treating the disorder is to stigmatize those who are experiencing it and label PTSD as a mental illness. You won't see combat-hardened Vets lining up for *that* recognition.

The subject of this particular project may hit uncomfortably close to home for many Veterans but perhaps combat Vets in particular. Combat Veterans; men who at some point in their lives had only a split-second, a mere heartbeat of a moment to react to some unexpected situation, to make a decision of life-affecting caliber who then had months or even years to think about and critically analyze the results of their actions from that one moment. As a result, every one of them at some point or another has had their token spot on some ledge: some even on the same one. Such men may spend the remainder of their lives wrestling with the consequences of whatever pushed them to that point, that ledge. And they are right; you can't possibly know how that feels unless you've been there. The gauntlet is thrown, defenses put into place, and the war at home begins.

As a society, we have no trouble accepting kids who choose to play particular contact sports that end up on the receiving end of multiple concussions who are then ripe for potential neurological deficiencies in their futures. We also acknowledge the plentiful stories about former professional football players who subsequently develop/are currently suffering neurological consequences of repeated concussions throughout illustrious careers. However, when men who have been to war present with PTSD, there is little to no empathy and very little understanding expressed by the public at large. Instead, echoing from various levels of insincerity, comments like *"What are they complaining about?"* and *"They knew what they were getting into when they joined"* tend to ring out. Yes, they knew they were going to battle, prepared for war but none of them knew about the war so many would be fighting after they returned.

Who is doing this judging? What makes it more acceptable for kids to knock each other in the head for the sake of a division championship or for grown men to dogpile a quarterback? How is it that we determine to question the claims of men who unhesitatingly served this country without question? Killed other men or seen their brothers die violent deaths? Were they not supposed to be affected? Were they not victims of traumatic circumstance? We'll just call them mentally ill, give them a few bottles of pills and send them on their way, forget about what sent them to that ledge in the first place.

Who does PTSD affect? The answer, most assuredly, is *'everybody'* whether people choose to believe that or not. World War II Veteran 'Babe' Heffron wrote in his memoir *'Brothers in Battle, Best of Friends'*:

> *"Any soldier who lived through combat, whether it was in 1776, 1861, 1918, 1944, any war, will never be entirely free of the war he fought. Some are just able to brush it off better than others."*

It cannot be said enough. Post-traumatic stress disorder can affect anyone for ANY traumatic or otherwise life-affecting event. However, in the military realm, PTSD is attributed to situations surrounding the combat experience. PTSD is not unique to select, chosen men or to specific branches of the military, wars or conflicts. It has affected many: too many. How did the medical community drop the ball for so many who've fought in the most recent conflicts and wars? How could anybody in good conscience say they didn't see this coming or that they didn't know, particularly since PTSD is something that has been recognized as happening as far back as the Civil War? Is it because it would cost so much to acknowledge and treat? The traumas of war don't affect just the military sector, either.

How about citizens? Families? Children? People cannot seem to comprehend the fact that the horrors and atrocities of war should be affecting everybody.

In the course of one specific week, the ugly suicide statistic regarding the number of combat Veterans taking their own lives reared its head in rapid succession. During the same span of time, several Marines hailing from one specific division had taken their own lives and within the same six months, an article appeared in the Florida Sun Sentinel. The article was a 'cut and dry' piece that publicized yet another study completed by the Veteran's Administration revealing,

"The likelihood of suicide among combat Veterans is greatest during the first two years following their leave of active duty."

The point to remember is that PTSD is a subjective matter. Not everybody is going to fit into the same diagnostic box. After all the decades that have passed since it was first recognized, maybe it's time to start thinking outside of the tidy clinical box and look at this from an entirely different angle.

⁇   In his New York Times best-seller Medal of Honor Peter Collier wrote, *"We reflect on what their lives might have been but will never be. Their sacrifice is our mandate; our challenge is to remember."* While Mr. Collier may have been referring specifically to Medal of Honor recipients, his statement rings true for ALL the members of our military.

"Their sacrifice is our mandate."

Virginia Tech Health and Performance Solutions posted an article written by Roberta Calhoun shared the following:

There've been legions of armchair warriors (i.e. people who've never served a day in military service in their lives) who somehow have felt qualified to pass judgment. Non-military people measure the military all the time, based on what they think they know from watching the news or playing video games, not by any experience. For such people, it's easy to make generalized comments and casually remark upon the issues and problems Veterans face. People comprising those armchair platoons feel certain military topics don't concern them or the happy lives they are enjoying civilian-wise. It's a concept seemingly beyond their comprehension, the fact that they can enjoy the lives they are living because somebody else has chosen to defend the Constitution.

War comes with various price tags. It's not only about the obvious or physical costs. Sometimes, the price of war has proven too high to pay and comes due long after all is believed to be said and done. Veterans have come home, surviving some of the most horrific and severe injuries ever imagined: injuries that in previous wars would have meant certain death. Indeed, these vets knew the risks going in, possibilities of things worse than death, yet they took the oath anyway. These Veterans spent months readying for war, training and preparing yet were not given even half the time to reintegrate when they came back to the world they left behind. How does a person prepare for life after the loss of limb(s) or ability? Those are the easy to see, *tangible* effects of war. What about all the things nobody can see like the mental and psychological issues? The fact is, those who did not lose limbs or abilities were still affected.

Refusing to see the obvious, many who've never experienced combat (or never enlisted, period) have little to no empathy. *"War is full of stupidity, nonsense, and death."* Of course it is. It's war. (If it were pretty, everybody would want in on it.) *"They knew what they were getting into. Nobody forced them to enlist."* Exactly. Since 1973, nobody has forced the less than 10% of the population who have voluntarily served to protect this country to sign any contract; and regarding those who have chosen to do so as Marines, that number is even less. These have been people, not expendable pawns or inconsequential lives to simply chalk up as collateral damage. The effect on their lives has in no way been simple, yet we treat their conditions that way after they come home. Is it any wonder why so many are reluctant to seek help?

War is an experience that affects the way Veterans live their lives long after their deployment ends. The world they leave behind (whether going to or returning from) all changes. It might be only four years, maybe eight (and sometimes beyond) but the role these men have trained for and were engaged in for so long, so intently forever changes them. Their lives of familiarity and routine disappear as they become whom they've expected to be and that effect doesn't melt away after they return home.

In the world they went to, it was often 'kill or be killed.' When empathy and humanity said, "no" reality from time to time said, "yes" and the people they helped? There was seldom any appreciation expressed. When they came home, maybe those Veterans just couldn't get back into the normal swing of things, couldn't reintegrate and as a result, experienced unexpected situations where things went beyond a stretch or two of hard luck. The familiarity and uniformity they had prepared for and lived in for two, three, six, seven deployments was suddenly gone.

While serving active-duty, there were assuredly times some of these Marines (and their Devil Docs and/or other supporting parties) felt especially compelled to make the occasional fire-watch confessional (fire-watch: think 'guard duty') and the person listening most likely hearing them out was another brother. This was how these men vented, how they addressed their doubts, uncertainties, and fears: how they existed: day in and day out. The phrase *'brother from another mother'* took on a completely new meaning. In the field, their lives depended on each other. They weren't out there just fighting for a cause or survival. They were also fighting for the guy next to, beside, in front and behind them.

Bonds forged in the theater of war are *indeed* that strong. When these men came home, all of that was gone. For those who needed it, medical science was supposed to fill the void; more often than not, by people who had never served, never experienced combat or loss. These people were supposed to step right up and make everything all better. What people on the outside looking in failed to recognize, (chose to forget) was that medicine is not and has never been an exact science. (Medical practices are called *practices* for a reason. Practice does *not* mean precision.) Perspective? Personal and professional perspectives do not matter as much as the main perspective: Veterans. When *their* reality changed, the whole world took on new meaning. What data did any stateside caregivers have to compare this with? But these Veterans' families knew. They knew that things weren't right when their Veterans came home. It didn't take much time at all for them to realize something had changed.

At least during the days of the Cold War (1945-1992) the

people 'back home' were more aware of what was going on in the world around them. They *had* to be: routine air raid drills were conducted, fallout shelters were put into place, canning and rationing of food were commonalities, planting Victory Gardens and saving paper bags were routine practice. Many older Americans can easily relate to if not actually share their memories of the Cold War Era, the Cuban Missile Crisis and give you their personal thoughts on Communism. Back in the day, everybody knew their neighbors and helped one another. In the world of today, we're a more pessimistic, severely disconnected and de-sensitized nation that has become overrun with political correctness and happy with merely existing behind closed doors instead of truly living.

Unless a person was ever affected directly, the nightly news reports about abductions or beheadings of individuals overseas haven't appeared to matter as much as they should.

"That sort of thing could never happen in this country. Why should it matter to me that some dictator committed mass genocide over in some country I've never been to? This is America. We have enough of our own problems to worry about." You'd think so.

In today's agenda, many people in our country take for granted things they've never had to worry about or worry about ever having taken away.

"Who cares about history? We all should, sure, shit happened. Let it go. Maybe we should fix what's wrong today instead of worrying about what happened a hundred years ago."

-JS

When we quit feeling and caring and began the frivolous, bullshit lawsuits and tiptoeing around the multi-cultures that this nation sprang from, there began the problems. The concept of a united country has already faded, and the current state of affairs probably has our ancestors rolling in their graves. In the process of attempting to please all the people all the time with politically and socially correct drivel, we lost track of who we should have been taking care of all along: our defenders. So many of us take for granted the freedoms we all enjoy without worrying about the price that has ultimately been paid.

We're all on paths to somewhere. Along those pathways are generous doses of cynicism with healthy portions of optimism and pessimism (and whatever other –isms lurking in the shadows) wrestling their way to the forefront as we make our way forward. The way any of those -isms will affect our lives depends on what the road looked like before we started; was it dirt? Gravel? Paved? *"Don't let the past control you?"* (Good luck with that, by the way.) As so many struggle with the forward motion, there are those who find themselves slipping backward, wrestling with demons that nobody told them about, nobody prepared them for. What about them? What about those individuals?

Each of us has a set of unique and significant moments defining our lives: some big promotion, a stint in the military, first child, college degree or conversely, the loss of a job, an automobile crash, or perhaps an unexpected divorce. Some people find it necessary to constantly reinvent themselves because of all the significant moments taking place in their lives. Following 1973 and the dissolution of the Draft, (but certainly not forgetting those who served before that time) there are many individuals whose moments include voluntary enlistment in the military in the USMC, the USN, USA, USAF or USCG and for some, consequently, four more letters: PTSD. To a boundless extent, the phrase '*You can't know unless you've been there*' continues to ring painfully true and in the end, we're all destined to become somebody's story, anyway.

In the fog of our overly complicated lives, there sometimes occur unplanned, unintended flickers of recognition: chance pieces of nearly faded memories, glimmers of otherwise repressed moments that randomly weave their way back into and through our current reality. Sometimes those unexpected thoughts, memories, and reflections find us in the wee small hours of the morning, or maybe right before we fall back asleep from the night before. Perhaps instead of a fleeting moment, it's a collection of unassuming minutes or maybe seemingly inconsequential 'a-ha' moments strung together that we've somehow subconsciously strung from the deep recesses of our mind. Whatever those moments are, they've been there waiting there the whole time for the right instant to reveal themselves. For some people, such unexpected moments are unwelcome and no time is ever right. For some, such feelings cannot be merely brushed away or ignored. How do we address that?

For the unlucky, when such stray impressions of seemingly ordinary (but significant) events flood their conscience unexpectedly, the process can be relentless. Something triggered such a moment into revealing itself. Whatever it is that causes a person to feel and hold on to such inexplicable feelings and emotion, it affects their entire view of life, not just that unexpected flash. Not everybody experiences such affecting flickers of their subconscious but many who do aren't always able to successfully rein them in. No matter what the explanation, once one of those unanticipated flashes occur, it can forever change a person and sometimes no matter how many counselors, resources or medications are made available, nothing is going to help that person manage the aftermath.

Not many upper-ranking members of the Marine Corps (or any other branch of the military for that matter) are fortunate in being able to say they've never lost a man under their command. A Marine's life is structured in a solid, essential routine of high expectations and successful completion of result-oriented missions. So then, what about those Marines who have lost somebody in their charge? Such losses have been conveyed as crushing, to say the very least. There are no words to describe the feeling other than guilt; guilt in not having been able to bring them all back home. *"Unless you've been there, you can't know what that feels like."*

Remember, PTSD is *not* military specific nor is it branch or gender specific. Many/any traumatic event from our everyday lives can lead to the development of PTSD, such as fire, natural disaster, mugging, robbery, motor-vehicle accident, plane crash, torture, kidnapping, life-threatening medical diagnosis, terrorist attack, and other extreme or life-threatening events: anybody can experience it.

-Part II-
Unwanted Gold

"Battles create and sometimes destroy heroes."

-K.D. Dickson

10 -WHY WE SHOULD *ALL* REMEMBER-
"Because forgetting should never have been an option in the first place."

There's no single or best way to honor the memory of a loved one who has gone too soon/taken from our lives. The manner in which anybody remembers is a delicate and subjéctive one (much the same as the demon-battling process.) There are just too many variables involved with any given circumstance to make the way we each remember somebody a uniform event. Nobody grieves or remembers in a single right or wrong way. If somebody doesn't go through Kübler-ross' five stages of grief in the exact order she wrote them, that doesn't give anybody else the right to condemn the way another chooses to or not to grieve.

It took more than a deep breath for many of Brandon Ladner's family and friends to feel comfortable in sharing personal stories about their Marine with the rest of the world. For some, even a deep breath was not preparation enough for the release of emotion they knew was going to follow.

For all the people who stepped forward to share stories about Brandon, there were twice as many who did/could not. Despite that fact, it took less than a year (nine months, actually) to pull this marine's story together. What you are about to begin is a collection of memories about a man who graced this world for only twenty-seven years. In less than a thousand days, this man accomplished more than most will in an entire lifetime.

This book was never meant to be 100%, all-encompassing when it came to Brandon Ladner. Mere words (no matter how descriptive) could never capture who this man truly was. Instead, from motorcycles to machine guns was meant to put a name and a face to a deplorable statistic: twenty-two. From motorcycles to machine guns was compiled so that those who were never blessed with knowing this marine could perhaps one day say, "I never met the man, but I know his story well."

The things we choose to take from a situation or experience, the very things we choose to hold on to most tightly cannot and do not accurately define who we are; only who we were at one time or another in our lives. All our life experiences ensure that we do not remain the same and remind us that everything is constantly changing. We can't take any of what we do or experience back, but we can move forward. We can learn, and we can remember. *"Remembering is easy. It's the missing part that's so hard."*

11-Honoring and Remembering-
June 11th, 2016
"You will always be because I will always remember you."

Several months after nearly all of the individual interviews about him had been transcribed and put into place, author and Veteran advocate TM Fitzgerald felt there was more that should be done to honor the legacy Brandon Ladner had left behind. There was still a tremendous healing process taking place in so many people, people whose lives Brandon had been such an enormous part of. There was also a delicate line between honoring the charmed life of a beautiful individual, determining if said honors were being recognized as what they were meant to be or considered salt being poured on a still fresh wound.

The idea for a special *'Rally, Roll, and Remember'* event was conceived to honor and remember the life of Sergeant Brandon Charles Ladner. Resulting from multiple phone calls, social media messages and Internet posts, a rapid influx of individual donations were directed to fulfill the specific purpose of Funds arrived from a veritable generation of Veterans from nearly every branch of service as well as from other Gold Star parents to sponsor an Honor and Remember flag in Brandon Ladner's name.

Though hundreds of such flags have been presented to Gold Star families across the country, many are still unfamiliar with the flag itself and its origins. The 'Honor and Remember' website shared the following information:

*"On December 29, 2005, Marine George Anthony Lutz
II (Tony) was killed by a sniper's bullet while he was on*

patrol in Fallujah, Iraq. His family and friends endured the shock, emotional agony and overwhelming loss that accompanied the news of Tony's death, just like the many families who have suffered the same tragedy.

In the months that followed Tony's funeral, his father, George, visited other families who had lost loved ones in the Iraq war. He began to sense that he had joined the ranks of a unique fellowship. These families were only the latest additions to a group that originated with the American Revolution, when the first soldiers to shed their blood for our freedom gave their lives.

George found another commonality among the families of fallen soldiers. After their grief had transitioned to numbness and finally to acceptance, many families wanted to know two things: their sacrifice was not in vain and the nation would never forget. These concerns led George on a quest to discover if there was a universally recognized symbol that specifically acknowledges the American service men and women who never made it home. To his surprise, he found nothing. Thus the Honor and Remember Flag was conceived."

In writing Brandon's story, author Fitzgerald wanted to ensure a special moment for Sergeant Ladner's family. Presenting an Honor and Remember flag seemed the natural thing to do. Made possible entirely out of generous donations from Veterans and Veteran's families across several generations, Brandon's flag presentation quickly turned from a simple idea to an incredible reality.

It was an event whose idea was initiated from several hundred miles away. The idea was to remember Ladner's life in a positive light in addition to raising general public awareness of that portentous statistic 'twenty-two'. The free-to-the-public rally was intended to connect people in the community with Veterans and encourage breaking the stigma surrounding PTSD. Additionally, this event was planned to help heal a family's still broken hearts and encourage the local community to connect with its Veterans and let them know that asking for help is okay.

"Veterans need to overcome the misconception that asking for help is a sign of weakness. It simply means we are human.

We can't get through this alone, and it's okay to admit that. At some point in time, we all took the oath. We took care of our military obligations when we were asked, so we need to take care of each other now."

-Eric Fort, Lone Warriors

On the evening of April 20th, 2016, approximately six hours northeast of Birmingham, Alabama, a UPS man was unaware of just how special the delivery he was about to make was to an anxiously anticipating customer. Chance made for author TM Fitzgerald to be

sitting in her office that night working on a rough draft of *From Motorcycles to Machine Guns* when the knock fell upon the door.

Briefly glancing at the return address on the parcel she'd just accepted, Fitzgerald knew instantly what she was holding her hands. Almost immediately upon receipt, Fitzgerald called Brandon's mother Renee to tell her what had just arrived. By the end of the week, Fitzgerald would once again be on her way to Alabama.

What follows is the original script from the initial portion of the PTSD rally held at the Alabama National Cemetery in Montevallo. The event was held in the same accommodations where Sgt. Ladner's committal services were held nearly two years prior. Initially, many believed the location was rather peculiar, but there was a specific reason as to why the rally was held here, as was explained by the following.

"In the words of Lone Warrior's CEO, former Marine Eric Fort, *"Every organization has its chosen mission: AMVETS, Mission 22, Leathernecks, Lone Warriors, etc. They all saw a need, a purpose..."* Due to many circumstances beyond my control, I suppose I may be considered an organization unto myself as well. I'm passionate about the missions I choose because I feel obligated to continue service to my country. I don't do the things I do for any recognition, but rather I do them for fellow Vets who need a little help or, as in the reason behind tonight's rally, I do what I do for those who can no longer tell their own stories.

The goal here this evening is multi-fold. It's not only to express gratitude to a young Marine's family for his voluntary, selfless service to this country but also to encourage a healthier awareness in the 'public at large' about an existing problem plaguing so many members of our military long after they return to familiar ground. We want to share some important information about a demon called PTSD, but first, I have three simple points to share about a knife, a concept, and a campaign.

It's interesting information that you may have never heard about regarding our Navy Seals and now you may be asking yourself, "How are these three things related? What do they have to do with Brandon Ladner or even the Marines for that matter?" Well, I'm about to tell you.

When Navy SEALS complete their training, two things happen. After each man successfully completes SEAL instruction, he's awarded his trident. The trident, of course, recognizes members of the Navy who've completed Basic Underwater Demolition/SEAL (BUDS) and SEAL Qualification Training (SQ). It's one of the most recognizable military badges of the Navy. However, the SEAL is also presented one additional item: a KA-BAR knife.

Now, as you may consider, one of the most important pieces of equipment that a SEAL may possess is his KA-BAR, but this knife is not a regular weapon. No, *this* particular knife is special in that inscribed on this knife is the name of a SEAL who died before him, *that* SEAL'S date of death and the place *he* died all inscribed on it. In this way, *that* knife links the new SEAL to the past. It serves as an inspiration to him in the future.

Six words expressed by the poet Wallace Bruce define this SEAL ritual best: *"The honor theirs...the duty ours."* It's not only our duty to learn from the past but also to remember it. Honoring and remembering our country's heroes: something to truly think about and something that should be encouraged by all. For those who do not learn from the past, are the ones destined to repeat it.

Tonight, we're gathered here rather curiously in Montevallo at this National Cemetery (of all places) for a specific reason. Tonight's location is important. This location, much like the KA-BAR knife given to each Navy SEAL upon graduation, is meant to serve as a reminder, as a connection to our own pasts. Look around you. Before leaving here tonight, I encourage each of you to walk among these stones and read the names. Take the time to speak those names out loud, because you don't know when last their names were spoken. Thank all of these Veterans who fought for our country.

We aren't here to mourn the death of a man but rather, to introduce *his* story, celebrate *his* life, learn from *his* existence, and to ponder. Tonight's event is about remembering Brandon Ladner, a young Marine who selflessly stepped forward and 'signed the line.' He took that oath to "defend this country against all enemies foreign and domestic" becoming one of the few, the proud but sadly, he also became part of a glaring statistic. Brandon became part of a number that has come to define the number of Veterans who take their own lives after they've returned from war. As of today, that number is twenty-two.

It's our hope that this special gathering here tonight will someday be remembered as a connection to the past, and maybe, just maybe, we'll be able to look back at *this* night as a cornerstone, as a moment of hope that maybe, we'll be able to say that we've seen the worst of that awful statistic. It's our hope that tonight may become a moment we can all look back on and be able to say, "Because of Brandon, somebody else's life was saved."

Now, you may wonder why I mentioned earlier that I'm an author. Well, before that, I'm an old Army Engineer but curiously enough, one who has taken to writing about Marines. I've published several books, many articles and am working on several projects right now, as a matter of fact in addition to Brandon's story. All of that just to share with you some wonderful news.

Many of you may know that at the end of last year, I established the honor of writing a biographical work about Brandon. It is my pleasure to announce that the final manuscript is nearly 100% complete and will be ready to submit to my editor within the next few months. (The manuscript for this book was completed on Brandon's 29th birthday, 2016.) Tonight, however, I'd like to take this opportunity in front of you all to present his mother, Renee a copy of the preliminary final draft. Brandon's book will be titled 'From Motorcycles to Machine Guns: The Very Necessary Story of Sgt. Brandon C. Ladner, USMC.'

Remember, my goal in writing has been to share the stories of Veterans who need a little help or can no longer tell their own. I became connected to Brandon Ladner because of another story I previously published about a Marine, one who also served in the 1/5 but who was KIA in October 2009. Brandon's book will be published within the next several months, so we are passing out these cards for you to keep as a reminder. The ultimate goal in writing Brandon's story was not only to honor his memory but with the hope that by sharing his life, perhaps others' lives might be saved, and empowering more people to have the courage to step forward and help those who have kept this country free.

Some of you may be asking yourselves about the connection between PTSD and the Marine we remember tonight: PTSD. Sergeant Ladner survived the war in Afghanistan but lost his personal fight with PTSD right here in Alabama. It's exactly what it sounds like. Brandon took his own life.

Too many people have been heard to remark, "I didn't know" or "I should have seen the signs."

Post-Traumatic Stress Disorder: PTSD…the other war that so many Veterans find themselves battling even after returning from war. That's not to say PTSD affects only Veterans, or only combat Marines or just members of the current military, period. 'Post trauma' means after any traumatic event experienced by ANYBODY.

Survivors of natural disasters, people who've endured severe car crashes, victims of sexual assault, and survivors of life-threatening illnesses…. ANYBODY can experience this life-affecting issue, but tonight, we're talking about a Veteran. Back a few months ago, official word was published that suicides related to PTSD had claimed the lives of more Veterans than those who have been killed in action in our recent wars. Translation: more have died here at home by their own hands than the number killed in combat.

PTSD isn't a new enemy; rather, it's one that has repeatedly reared its ugly head, one that has been recognized as far back as the Civil War. It's a subjective disorder and our culture has made it nearly a disgrace for a Veteran to step forward and admit they may have a problem or ask for help. We want to make this less of an issue, less of a stigma and encourage these men (and women) to step forward. Asking for help is not a sign of weakness. We all need a little help to get by now and again, and as Veterans, we need to take care of our own.

We've heard the terms shell shock, neurosis, psychosis…but what is PTSD exactly? PTSD is a common and potentially debilitating condition. It's not something 'just in their heads.' It may start out subtle at first, lasting for months or many years, with triggers that can bring back memories of the traumatic event and be accompanied by intense emotional and physical reactions. Some of the symptoms include flashbacks, nightmares, anxiety, and depression any of which can present itself at any given moment in time.

Treatment is subjective and depends on the symptoms that show up. Currently, treatment can include different types of psychotherapy or as quite often the case, different combinations of medications are used to manage the depression and anxiety that often accompany it. Many resources are available for people affected by this disorder, but too many do not or don't know how to access them. Approximately 5% of people in the US suffer from PTSD, and 8% of the population has had it at some point in their lives. Veterans are the focus here tonight, but many don't know where or how to get help beyond the VA.

Brandon Ladner was the absolute last person in the world that anybody would have suspected would take his own life. Indeed, PTSD is that powerful. As people on the outside looking in, we need to raise awareness and offer our hands, not ignore or push away the fact that this is a real affliction. The unit Brandon was a part of, the 1/5, has suffered, to date, over a dozen deaths to suicide from the same deployment. That's over a dozen young men who survived fighting a war on foreign soil only to return and take their own lives back here, at home. Brandon was not the first, nor sadly enough, was he the last. The 1/5 isn't even the only unit with such a massive loss of life due to the effects of PTSD.

What good are tributes or flowers to a person *after* they are gone? Those things aren't meant so much for those who are gone as they are meant as reminders for the living, forcing us to realize what honor there is in being so remembered by friends and battle comrades, years, even decades after a person's life ends, but what about those who remain? What about those left behind?

That brings me to this portion of tonight's event. I'm not an official representative of the H&R Organization, nor am I appointed by anybody for any specific detail or missions regarding such. I am a

Veteran's advocate, and I have a curious tendency of showing up in places where Veterans gather.

I'm sure everybody here tonight is familiar with the black POW/MIA flag, but let me ask this. How many are familiar with Combined Federal Campaign 92995? CFC #92995 is a national crusade of the Honor and Remember organization; a group founded by Goldstar Father George Lutz, Sr. who lost his son, Cpl George Lutz, II in December of 2005. CFC 92995 is his vision one that strives to recognize the thousands who have bravely made the ultimate sacrifice while preserving the freedoms of this country. This campaign is not limited to any one war, incident, or time-period. It's simply a movement created out of a father's grief and desire to 'have something to hold on to,' something that represented the price that his son and thousands of others have paid.

The Honor and Remember Flag was conceived *"To establish a tangible national symbol of gratitude as a visible public reminder to all Americans; perpetually recognizing the sacrifice of our military fallen heroes and their families."* As we all know, Brandon Ladner was fighting a different kind of war and despite his return from Afghanistan; he never truly made it all the way home. We not only wanted to share his story but also wished to honor and celebrate his life and the fact that he voluntarily served his country as a United States Marine. Joel Doss is here to explain the symbolism of the flag.

The Honor and Remember Flag's design is distinctive, yet simple. Each detail on the flag symbolizes an important part of the overall meaning of the flags message. The Red Field represents the blood spilled by brave men and women in America's military throughout our history, who willingly gave their lives so that we all could remain free.

The Blue Star represents active service in military conflict. This symbol originated with World War I, but on this flag, it signifies service through all generations from the American Revolution to present day.

The White Border beneath and surrounding the gold star recognizes the purity of sacrifice. There is no greater price an American can pay than to give his or her life in service to our country.

The Gold Star signifies the ultimate sacrifice of a warrior in active service who will not return home. Gold reflects the value of the life that was given.

The Folded Flag signifies the final tribute to an individual life that a family sacrificed and gave to the nation.

The Flame is an eternal reminder of the spirit that has departed this life yet burns on in the memory of all who knew and loved the fallen hero.

We will always honor their selfless sacrifice and remember them individually by name.

Additionally, aside from conveying the fact that *'Nothing is gained without some risk,'* author Louis L'Amour penned the following. *"There are two kinds of people: those who wish and those who will. The world and all its goods will always belong to those who will."* Brandon was part of those who will...still. Of all our warriors whom we honor and remember, I now share these words from II Corinthians 9:7 *"They gave much and knew not that they gave at all."*

Brandon Ladner gave himself to the world, and as one of the less than ten percent who served, he stepped up to protect this country, people he never met, and people he would never know. He also saw and experienced things on foreign soil so that we might never have to worry about those things here. He, like so many others, deserves to be remembered. In leaving here tonight, say to yourselves this: "I will learn more about PTSD, encourage my Vets to seek help, and always, always remember: they went to fight 'over there' so that war may never come here."

I've been given to know about the celebrated bond that Marines share, one across generations, a brotherhood of nearly legendary proportion. The Marines steadfastly believe in and practice the warrior ethos: "*Leave no man behind.*" I've studied and learned in great detail about the fabled beast that is Marine. Brandon ultimately lost his life for this country. He represented America as a United States Marine on foreign soil, but he left this world a United States Marine. Brandon was a giver, and though he did not know it, he was still giving the night he left this world, and is giving still. Let's keep alive this Marine's memory by reaching out and helping our heroes who are still struggling. If you know anybody who served and is having problems, is dealing with PTSD, struggling...be the one who offers a hand. Help them to help themselves. Let them know that it's okay to reach for that hand. "*They all need to be remembered.*"

The Marines have an unofficial motto: "*No greater friend, no worse enemy.*" Long before George Lutz the younger ever thought about becoming a Marine, the Corps gave the world a Latin phrase to consider: "*Semper Fidelis; always faithful.*" Concerning CFC #92995, tonight I give you another: "*Semper Conmemoro: always remember.*" To that, I also add this: "*Numquam Obliviscar: never forget.*"□

-Such Good Men-
(Adaptation of Michael Norman's 'These Good Men')

I know why men who have been to war yearn to reunite. Not to tell stories or look at old pictures, not to laugh or even weep. Comrades gather because they long to be with the men who once acted their best, with men who suffered and sacrificed, men who were stripped raw, all the way down to their humanity.

They didn't choose one another. They were delivered by Fate and songs of war but they know each other in a way they know no other man. They have never given anyone such trust. They were each willing to guard something more precious than one another's life. They each have carried one another's reputation: the memory of each man that was lost. It was part of the bargain they all made, the reason they were all so willing to die for one another.

They cannot know where they are headed tomorrow, these warriors of ours. Theirs are not perfect friendships. No, those are the province of legend and myth. A few friends will drift far from one another now, sending back only the occasional word and they each know that one day, even those will fall to silence. But some will remain close....and a couple, perhaps always at hand.

As long as they have memory they will think of them every day. And each of them will be certain that when their time comes to leave this world, their last thoughts will not be just of family but also of battle buddies: all of them, their brothers in arms. These were all such good men.

"There will come a time when you believe everything is finished. Yet that will be just the beginning."
-Louis L'Amour

12-August 2016-
Mission22 Memorial Update

At the beginning of August 2016, author Fitzgerald was given to learn more about the organization Mission22 by way of an unexpected announcement. First of all, what is Mission22 and how does this organization relate to Brandon Ladner?

> *"The number of soldiers who don't survive life as a civilian is a crisis of its own and a mission is underway that's working to change that."*
>
> -Jason Brick, 2014

Elder Heart partnered with the publicity firm CP+B and created Mission22. Mission22 was formed *"To bring mindfulness of the challenges facing returning Veterans every day."* Their goal utilized the phenomena of social media to promote their campaign against the war at home that nobody wanted to talk about: Veteran suicide. In his 2014 article, Brick further explained the goal of Mission22.

> *"Using hashtags and media support, the effort encourages everybody to post images of the number 22 — from street signs, to house numbers, to custom art — on their social media and tell people why they're doing it. Mission22 is encouraging awareness and soliciting funds toward two goals. First, they want to expand their offerings of resources for Veterans families and communities to "save the 22" Veterans who might otherwise take their own lives this year. Secondly, they want to place a memorial in Washington DC to memorialize these home front victims of wars, who gave their lives for their country just as surely as did those killed in action."*

Information from the Mission22 website itself explained best who the organization are and what their goal is: http://www.mission22.com

> *"Elder Heart is the 501C3 (a non-profit organization) behind Mission 22. It is comprised of Delta Force and Special Forces operators Tom Spooner, Magnus*

Johnson, and Mike Kissel. Because of their personal battles with PTSD and TBI, they have each made it their mission to raise awareness, enlist support, and end Veteran suicide in America."

The following information was also obtained from their website and further explains *'The War at Home'* monument.

"There are memorials dedicated to the fallen warriors of nearly every major conflict in our country's history. These memorials remind us of the sacrifice, honor those we've lost, and help tie civilian to soldier. Yet, there is no national monument for those who have fallen in the war against Veteran suicide. With your support, we're going to build one. Let's raise a monument—and, with it, awareness. We'll be working with community leaders in locations like Washington, D.C. and New York City to create a permanent exhibit that pays tribute to the 22."

"The 'War at Home Memorial' will be a mobile monument. It will move around the United States, calling a new city home every couple of years. This will allow its impact to grow with each new location, ensuring that more cities and communities are able to honor all of their Veterans. Each steel plate will be created in the likeness of a real American Veteran who lost the battle with PTSD. Details about their lives and service will be described in an inscription located at the base of each plate."

The unexpected announcement came by way of Brandon's mother Renee, who shared the fact in a post on Facebook that Brandon's image was one chosen to be part of the memorial.

"My Son's Memory will live forever. Thank you Mission22, TM Fitzgerald, NASCAR, all the wonderful people who have put together the 22 hikes, the people who walk the hikes, TIME Magazine for sharing my sons battle with PTSD which ultimately took his life, all Brandon's friends and all our family members who have been here for us through this bigger than life heartache that I/ WE carry every single day. Without all of you, we wouldn't have or be able to continue to HONOR AND REMEMBER the beautiful soul that is my son. I want to share the amazing project that MISSION22 has put together to honor and remember Veterans who have lost their battle with PTSD. This organization has chosen twenty-two Veterans and is putting together a monument made of steel plates of silhouettes of our loved ones who have been lost to suicide. When complete, the monument will be set up in Bandera, Texas. There will be plaques naming each silhouette and a biographical account of each Veteran. Mission22 has completed sixteen plates with just six more to go. I will post more details when the memorial is complete and in place. Dedication details will follow when I'm notified. Thank you all
Sgt. Brandon Ladner's Family

-PHOTO GALLERY-

"The most important thing is to enjoy your life - to be happy - it's all that matters."

-Audrey Hepburn

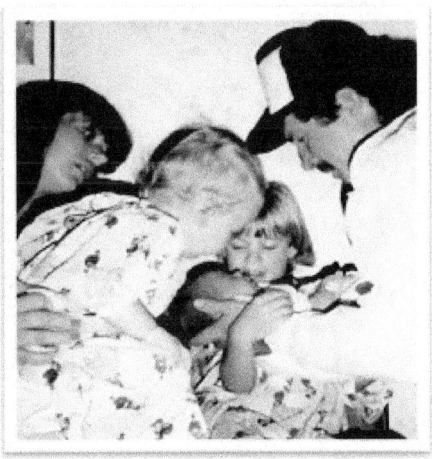

Welcoming baby brother Brandon into the world.

Brandon's First Bike

Marine Corps Graduation

Brandon's brother Chris

Afghanistan

California

Brandon visiting his sister in Hawaii on R&R

Drinking a signature dirty martini

St. Patrick's Day celebration

Arriving in California from Afghanistan

Hurricane evacuation, on our way to Nashville

Brandon and big sister Nicole singing by the fire

Proud Mama and her two youngest

Brandon with Marine brother Cole Wilson

Welcome Home From Deployment Surprise Party

Another day in the country

'Present in spirit'

The War at Home' memorial, Bandera, Texas 2016

Alabama National Cemetery, Montevallo Alabama

June 11, 2016

In Their Own Words

-Douglas Sinclair, USMC-

"I miss the Marines. Life on the outside makes you wonder, 'Why did we give so much yet get so little in return?'"

"My family had moved to Alabama somewhere around 1999, but I didn't meet Brandon Ladner (either through my brother or my best friend TJ, Brandon's brother-in-law) until a few years later, around 2000 or 2001. I have to say, I thought he was hilarious right from the start."

"You asked for adjectives I'd use to describe Brandon? Well," Mr. Sinclair paused "-badass is one of the first words that comes to mind. Brandon was one of the toughest guys I've ever known. I mean, with regard to his physical attributes, he was *definitely* intimidating, but as far as his personality, he was a very aid back kind of guy. Nothing seemed to bother him, not even the little shit. He was pretty easy-going but when he found stupidity in something, he became the Hulk. That's the best way I'd describe him. If you happened to piss him off, you'd better get out of his way. I mean, Brandon was as strong as shit. I remember talking with another friend of ours about how one time the two of them were just wrestling around and Brandon picked him up and threw him through a glass table. It impressed me when I heard about that."

"The table incident might make him seem like he was some hard-assed individual but Brandon certainly wasn't like that. He was giving and selfless in so many ways. Sometimes it seemed he cared more about other people than he cared about himself. If he was down to the last dollar in his pocket and you needed it, he wouldn't think anything of giving it to you."

"Brandon was a huge Alabama fan. I mean, it was '*Roll Tide*' all the way and all the gear he could get his hands on. Myself, I'm an LSU man and absolutely hate Alabama. There was this one game or another that we'd been watching where Alabama almost pulled off a win: almost. Well, LSU started pulling ahead, and Brandon had about given up on Alabama, so he was all like, '*Let's go get a beer.*' I mean, he was such a die-hard fan. We never let that interfere with our friendship though. Once you were friends with Brandon, you were friends for life."

"I think a lot about how his sister Nicole and I were the ones who took him up to the recruiting station in Birmingham. The fact that he's gone now, well I hate that I introduced him to the machine that led him down the path. I mean, I physically took him to the recruiter's office." Mr. Sinclair took an audible breath and was silent a moment before he continued.

"I was already a Marine and had been home on recruiter assist. At the time, Brandon seemed like this goofy, naïve kid who didn't know what was going on. One day, he and I went to the recruiters' office together. Of course, him being such a huge Alabama fan, he had on his stupid Alabama hat. The recruiters already knew me, of course, but wanted to know who Brandon was. One of them asked him, "So you want to be a Marine?" and Brandon was all 'Yes sir!' The Gunny proceeded to tell him, "How about you take that fucking hat off?" Brandon immediately removed his hat and decided he was going to become a Marine."

"Brandon wanted to go infantry, but he'd also wanted to go to go on his class trip for school. Long story short, he went on the class trip and in the process missed his infantry slot. However, you know, no matter their MOS, *every* Marine is an infantryman first, right? Once Brandon got in, he was all up into what he was supposed to do. That's pretty much his story. I'll never forget how Gunny acted toward him that day. I guess Brandon appreciated the bluntness because he became a United States Marine."

"When I first found out about what happened with Brandon, I was still living in Alabama. I was on my way to work when I first heard the news. TJ (Brandon's brother-in-law) called and told me. I thought he was lying. I mean, you have to understand. Brandon loved life no matter what was going on. He was such a giving, caring, kind of guy. I didn't believe TJ at first, so I immediately signed onto Facebook to check things out. That's when it hit me. 'This shit is real.' (Facebook, can you believe that? I mean, that's what we do for confirmation. It was real.) I don't think we even ended up going to work that day."

"I have to admit, before Brandon died, I didn't know what twenty-two a day meant, but I sure can relate now: twenty-two a day." Doug paused. "That's insane, ridiculous, and deep. You want to talk about culture shock? When I got out of the military, I went from the rigid, structured atmosphere of the Marine ethos back to a world where few had similarly served. People who've never served can't relate to or understand what I'm talking about. Unless you've been there, you can't *possibly* know. I don't know what our leadership is doing about twenty-two but they need to talk to the Vets who've been there and listen for some good, solid, feedback."

"As for myself, I was basically pink-slipped out of the military. We had two weeks of bullshit resume writing classes but when I was all the way out, I was ignorant of any programs available to Veterans. There's just so much shit out there that they don't tell you about. Where are all the advocates *after* you leave the active military component? Once you EAS (End of Active Service/get discharged), nobody wants anything to do with you."

"Even though there's so much information out there, (on Facebook especially) we still need more people advocating for Veterans. As far as my own issues, I've gotten help from the VA. I've been out three years and resorted to substance abuse and a shitty life outside the Marines. I'm just now learning about resources. The Marines taught me how to be a leader, to manage people and then when I got back out into the real world, it was nothing but struggle. I went to work, thought I was doing my job and the next thing I knew, HR was pulling me into the office. '*Mr. Sinclair, we need to talk.*'"

"I'm looking at all of this from a different kind of perspective. Two years before I EAS'd, the USMC implemented a suicide prevention program. I was the 'go-to' guy who had to educate other Marines on the matter. Even though I was that guy and had all the knowledge, all the tools, I could still sometimes relate to Marines like Brandon. At the same time, I had the tools to use but," He paused. "-I gave the Corps ten years of my life. When they're done with you, they don't prepare you for everyday life back in the civilian world."

"At my first job after I got out, I remember getting mad at this girl I worked with. I mean, she had a degree and all the proper qualifications I guess, but she had nothing as far as true leadership ability. Of course, I was holding her to a military standard, the Marine standard and she'd never served. Let's just say that coming out of the Marines, my tolerance for stupidity was not high."

"Transition's been rough. When I was about to get out of the Marines, I was excited at first, but let me tell you, the process could have been a hell of a lot easier. We have to have such self-control in the PC world that we've become: have to keep check not only on what you say, but how you say it as well. You can't just punch people in the face, so to speak." Mr. Sinclair chuckled slightly at his own comment. "You're military," Sinclair added as he interviewed with Fitzgerald. "-you know what I mean."

"I had a good job when I first got out but long story short, I quit. I hit a low spot in my life and became addicted, and well, I eventually came around to thinking that maybe all the stuff I was going through was on some level how I was experiencing my own PTS. I'm getting help now, though. I go to groups, I go to counseling, participate more in things. Up until about seven months ago, things were pretty shitty for me." Mr. Sinclair took a deep breath. "I miss the Marine lifestyle. It makes you wonder, why did we care to give so much yet get so little in return?"

☐

-Roundtable I:
Birmingham, November 2015-

"He always had your back. I felt I owed him a debt for serving our country."

On Thursday evening, November 05, 2015, what had been intended as being the first in a series of 'one-on-one' interviews turned into an engaging roundtable discussion as a number of people gathered and seated themselves around an ordinary dining room table. Before they began, glasses were raised to honor the memory of 1/5 Marine, Sgt. Brandon Charles Ladner. The drink of the hour? Dirty martinis, of course, which were Brandon's favorite. After an unexpected round of dour faces, the first individual up to bat was one of Brandon's closest friends.

When asked how the two of them first met, Jamy Wayman only had to think briefly before answering.

Jamy Wayman: "I met Brandon through a mutual friend of ours, I believe sometime around 2005. I happened to be recovering from a motorcycle wreck and was just getting back into the swing of things. It wasn't long after I met Brandon that the three of us started hanging out pretty regularly. We did everything together."

"I knew Brandon before he'd enlisted in the military. When I found out he'd signed to go, I was so psyched for him. I knew he'd make a great Marine." Jamy paused. "One thing that stands out about all that in particular though was Brandon's transformation. I mean, like I said, I knew him before he went to boot camp but when he came home, everybody was like, "Whoa!" You have to know, Brandon was already a big guy but the Marines had trimmed him down and toned him up. When he came home, he was cut like crazy. I mean, they had him looking like how you'd picture a Marine was supposed to look. It wasn't so much about him leaving for boot camp as it was seeing him after he came home and seeing what the military had done to him. Brandon was one proud Marine."

"We're talking about a guy who was absolutely hilarious. Brandon was that guy who could make everybody in the room laugh. He'd do anything for his friends, too. Let me tell you about this one New Year's Eve party. I'd just gotten out of a bad relationship so of course, we all went out drinking. Long story short, I drank too much. Sure enough, I was feeling horrible and was all like, 'I'm about to get sick' so I went into the bathroom and proceeded to throw up. Well, Brandon comes in behind me with this bottle of champagne. I have no idea where he got it from, but he popped the cork, put it in front of me and told me. *'Here man, drink some of this. It'll make you feel better.'* I told him, 'Dude! Get out of here!' So he starts chugging the bottle himself. I started laughing and throwing up at the same time (which I know, sounds pretty gross) but Brandon finally set the bottle down and said, *'Dude. I'm not going to let you throw up all by yourself,'* stuck his fingers down his throat and started throwing up in the sink."

"So there we were; both of us throwing up in the bathroom and dying because we were laughing so hard. It was a horrible experience, but it was one of those times with Brandon that I'll never forget. I couldn't believe he did that. Between me, Brandon, and Johnny, there are so many little stories I could tell."

"This is hard to explain, but something I want to share. A lot of times, Brandon would randomly blurt out the word 'Red!' and the rest of us would immediately respond, 'Yeah!' Then, there was the whole 'P' thing we'd do. 'P, man' which meant, 'I'm being serious' as in 'friendship with a 'P' on the end. We have friendship with a 'P.' We'd be out somewhere and Brandon would be across the room and suddenly shout out, *'Do something!'* and make the symbol for the letter 'P.' It's hard to explain all those little things he did, things nobody else will ever understand but they're part of what made Brandon who he was. There's so many, an absolute ton. That's just how we rolled."

After the good-humor at the table had quieted, the next question took a 180-degree turn.

"What were the first thoughts that came to mind when you heard what had happened to Brandon?"

Jamy who, while first to respond, did not speak immediately. Instead, he turned deep in thought. When he finally spoke, his voice wavered briefly.

"When I first heard," Jamy paused. "-I couldn't believe it. I was beyond shocked. I mean, I remember *exactly* what I was doing when I found out." Searching his thoughts very carefully, Jamy continued, his voice more subdued. "I was at work when I received a text from a friend. '*What happened to Brandon?*' Of course, I immediately responded, "What are you talking about?" My friend texted back, '*You haven't heard?*' so I signed onto Facebook. That's how I found out he had passed."

Jamy looked at his hands briefly before taking a deep breath and continuing. "Being personally affected by that statistic, the number 'twenty-two' sickens me. I hate it. It isn't fair how our Vets are treated after they get out. I feel like the VA did Brandon wrong. It makes me so angry that we lost him." Pausing again, Jamy's voice softened. "We need to educate people in this country so nobody can say, 'I didn't know.' We need to wake people up and look at what our guys are going through, especially after they come home. We train them to do what they have to do 'over there' and then pull them back into the regular world-," With a tremendous display of emotion, Jamy let his voice trail silent. After thinking for a moment, he shared the following.

"You had to know Brandon to get who he was. He was a great guy and loyal friend. I mean, he was so goofy and would do such stupid, goofy things that would catch you off guard. He'd do outrageous things in public just to make you laugh. It made no difference to him; he didn't care who you were, where you were or who you were with. He was always a man on a mission. You couldn't ask for a better friend than what you got in Brandon."

"He loved bonfires. When he'd decide to have a party, he'd call everybody he knew and would be all like, '*Come over tonight. We're gonna have a bonfire.*' The first time I ever went to one of his bonfires,

I thought, 'Okay. A bonfire: like a little patio thing' but no: not Brandon. He'd made this great big, enormous fire pit that was about eight or ten feet across all lined with blocks. It was massive. We burned stuff until three or four in the morning, just sitting around and talking. Those were some of the best times, sitting by that pit having ordinary conversations and drinking beer. One time, there ended up being like thirty, forty people out there when the neighbors decided it was time for us to stop." Jamy laughed and shook his head. "Those were some good times over there."

Chris Stalls: "Believe me, stopping you guys that night wasn't my idea." Stalls turned to explain what had happened. "They'd all get together out there like that quite often. I'm one that usually goes to bed early. Well, the way my house is set up, my room faced where they'd have their bonfires going on. Sometimes I'd look out the window about six in the morning and see somebody staggering across the yard, and then I'd see Brandon come by a little later." Stalls smiled, shaking his head at the memory. "Brandon and his bonfires..."

Jamy: "There were times around one or two in the morning when we'd run out of stuff to burn and have to run back into the woods to chop a tree down or pull in a woodpile from back there: anything we could find to keep the fire going."

Chris: "I'd be at work, and Brandon would call, '*Chris, can you bring home some pallets?*' I'd tell him sure and go drive out behind Publix (grocery chain) and throw a couple in the back of the truck."

Jamy: "Here's another thing. We'd all just be sitting around, and somebody would get Brandon to start rapping. Every time we'd go out, he'd get a little buzz going and we'd get him to do it. He was really good at it, too."

Renee: "I don't know how he could think that fast. Everything just went together. He was so amazing at it. I can't even think that fast."

Chris: "He never had to think about it. He just did it."

Renee: "They call that 'free stylin', right? When Brandon came home from Afghanistan, I'd picked him up from the airport. On our way back to the house, he just started doing it off the top of his head. He knew I'd always wanted him to do it for me but he never would. When he started rapping that day, I was like, 'Oh my Gosh!' and nearly wrecked the car."

Jamy: "I got him to do it one time at some other party we were at, and everybody turned around and was like, 'What's going on?' He was that good." Jamey paused as his thoughts turned back to his friend. "I've never met another person more proud of being a Marine than Brandon himself. He was super proud."

"For my bachelor party, we went to Crab Island in Destin. The first thing, Brandon spotted a couple of Marine flags flying over on this other boat. *'We have to go talk to those guys.'* I was like, 'Alright buddy, let's go.' We went over and he meshed right in. It was so crazy to witness."

Renee: "Johnny had us rolling one night talking about the stuff he and Brandon had done in school. Somebody did something to one of Brandon's friends and there went Brandon, straight over to the Winn-Dixie parking lot. He jumped into a car and started beating on the guys who were in the wrong. Brandon always had his friend's backs no matter what."

Jamy: "My brother-in-law and Brandon met up one night at the bar where there was this other guy who was being a real ass. The bar's bouncer was getting pretty fed up, so Brandon went up to the bouncer and asked him, *'You want me to take care of that guy for you?'* The bouncer told Brandon if he took care of the trouble-maker, he'd take care of Brandon's bar tab so of course, Brandon destroyed the guy; knocked him clean out. I wasn't there to witness that one but I heard the story." Jamy paused as he smiled. "Brandon was never afraid to stand up to anybody."

Renee: "He loved scaring the hell out of people, too. Brandon hid behind doors all the time, jumping out when you'd least expect it. Oh my Gosh, right up to when he passed away, he was still jumping out and scaring the wits out of people. He'd scare the daylights out of you but make you laugh at the same time. Brandon was exceptionally funny."

Jamy: "He made it to my bachelor party but," Jamy stopped. "-Brandon was supposed to be *in* my wedding, too." Jamy sat back as he continued "For some of my wedding photos, we took Brandon's Marine portrait and placed it on an easel alongside my groomsmen. It's one of my favorite pictures taken by the lake. I remember sitting there that morning just imagining, talking and having a regular conversation with him." Jamy paused before adding, "I can still hear his voice."

Regina: "I still look out the front door waiting to see his truck sitting across the street."

Jamy: "he loved that truck, too didn't he? I told him not to buy it but he wanted it so bad. So of course, he ended up getting it."

After a lively discussion about the truck Brandon had recently purchased, the next person to allow himself to be interviewed was neighbor Chris Stalls.

Chris: "When I first met Brandon, he was just coming back from Afghanistan. He was a respectful, always willing to help-you-out kind of guy; would help anytime with anything. He always had your back. I often felt like I owed him a debt for serving our country. I thought a lot of him, like he was my own son. Brandon was a special person."

"Like Jamy said, there's so much to say, to tell about him, so many little things. I could sit here and think about this all night long." Chris paused as he took a slow sip of beer. "Fire pits- he'd asked me if it'd be alright if he built a pit for a bonfire. I'm with you, Jamy on this one. When he asked about that, I never thought anything of it, maybe a small fire on the patio. I had no idea it was going to be as big as it was. It was more like a ten-foot square hole in the ground complete with crossties and cement blocks. I'd only been expecting something the size of this table but no," Chris laughed "-though I have to admit; it was top of the line. I was impressed. I just wish all the neighbors could have enjoyed it as much as we did."

"Brandon was so spontaneous. Remember St. Patrick's Day? We'd planned on going out to the bars that night so I went over to pick him up. I didn't have a green shirt for the night and of course, Brandon had one and asked if I wanted to wear it. 'Man, why don't you spike your hair?' Now, those who know me know that I'm particular about how I wear my hair. Brandon didn't think I'd do it. I surprised him. 'Okay.' 'No, you won't do it.' 'Yes I will.' 'You ain't gonna spike your hair.' 'Yes I will. Give me the damn gel.' So we went in and spiked my hair."

Renee: "You couldn't even move it. His hair was *way* too long to be spiked, but they had it sticking way up there."

Chris: "It took about three days to get all that gel washed out, too. I don't know what he used, some stuff called Bed Head or Freaze-something."

Switching gears after the St. Patrick's Day story, Chris began talking about another incident.

Chris: "Brandon hadn't had his truck very long before we had to go up back behind the house and give him a tow. You have to understand; there's miles of roads back there. We finally found Brandon and his buddies after hours of searching but after we found them, we soon figured out that we didn't have anything to pull them up out of the mud with. All they had were extension cords (of all things) so what did they decide to do? Brandon and Mitch tied them up to the truck and commenced to pulling. Of course, those cords snapped in no time at all. Brandon locked the hubs, and we had to 4-wheel them up out of there."

Renee: "Brandon had been trying to pull them out. Mitch had been standing behind the truck and in the process of them trying to get free, Brandon bumped him and he fell into the mud. Eventually, they just decided to leave the truck and go back to the house. Of course, come next morning, the cops came knocking. Brandon answered the door, saw who it was and yelled up to Mitch, *'There's somebody at the door for you.'* He went back to his room and shut the door. He didn't want to talk to the cop."

Chris: "I took Brandon to his first NASCAR race over in Talladega. We didn't have tickets, but I wasn't worried about getting in. (When all was said and done, we ended up with two tickets, an extra $25.00 and beer so all was good.) We went over there and ended up having a great time. The next year, we went back for the big race and we were in the same predicament as the year previous; no tickets, but nobody was worrying."

"I was wearing a ton of Mardi Gras beads that time and one set consisted of a pair of boobs. Brandon and I had walked off looking for the bathrooms and had left the girls sitting up in the stands. While we were walking, this woman came up and saw all my beads. Now understand," Chris leaned forward with a grin. "-there was nothing this woman was gonna show me that would have me giving up any of my beads; I mean nothing. I was nice, but no. I wasn't giving up my beads. She asked, 'What do I have to do to get some of those beads?' Like I said, there wasn't anything but Brandon starts saying, 'Come on Chris. Give her some. Give her some of your beads.'"

Regina: "When they came back up to the stands, Brandon was laughing so hard. 'You're not going to believe what just happened.'" Regina recapped Chris' story. "I remember we had beer when we walked in but by the time the race was over, it was all gone. I mean, we had zero, so as we walked back to the truck, we started hollering 'We ran out of beer. Anybody have any beer? We have a Marine here and he's out of beer!' As soon as we said 'Marine,' throngs of people started walking to us. You see, on Sundays, it used to be a dry county around the track but they recently changed that. We were determined to carry on with our celebrating and ended up driving all the way over to Jefferson County on a beer run."

"Our little party hadn't ended at the track. We went home, turned on the music and started dancing, determined to continue having a great time. We must have partied until two or three that next morning. Brandon was so happy. I mean, every one of us was tore down to the floor."

Renee: Brandon's mom had been sitting at the table, quietly taking in the stories about her son as she interjected, "He just didn't know. He didn't know what was going on within himself. The PTSD was already there."

Chris: "I wish he'd have never left the Corps. I know he missed it every day."

Regina: "He sure did. I remember he came over to the house one time and started pulling up videos on YouTube about Afghanistan to show us stuff that had happened over there. 'Look at that!' he'd say. 'That's the real thing!'"

Chris: "I don't think he was happy as a civilian."

Renee: "I know he wasn't. He'd planned on reenlisting."

Regina: "I agree. I mean, I didn't understand that at first. I guess Brandon was one of those guys who felt *more*, I mean *'once a Marine, always a Marine.'* That definitely was him. It was so deeply embedded in his ideals."

Chris: "He was a hard-charger, that's for sure. I'd heard all about Parris Island from other Marines I've known prior to Brandon, and those guys were some tough sons of bitches, but in Brandon- I could see it in him: the Marine. There was nobody more proud of wearing the uniform. He took pride, and looked real good in those dress blues."

Regina: "He gave so much of himself."

Chris: "He was *always* there whenever I needed anything."

At the beginning of the round-table discussion, Regina McNeal had been hesitant in answering any questions presented to the group. However, as the evening progressed and her initial apprehension overcome, she began to talk more and shared her experiences. When the question was presented asking how she had learned the news about Brandon, she quietly explained.

Regina: "I was the one who found him."

Chris Stalls cut in. "Regina and I had been in North Carolina for a funeral and had made it back here to the house around one in the morning. I'd been driving all day in some hard rain so when we got closer to home, Regina took over. I still had a trip to make to Chattanooga the next day and was dreading it, so I kicked back and fell asleep."

Regina: "We got home and just left everything out in the car and went straight to bed. As I woke Chris up to tell him we were home, we'd noticed the lights were on over at Brandon's."

Chris: "It was late, like I said but we'd noticed the door open and lights on over there. That in and of itself was strange, but I just thought Brandon was up late studying or something. He was always up early for his job at the post office. One time, he told me, *'If you're up and you see my truck over here, call me. I'm late for work.'* Remember, I'd only had like four or five hours of sleep to this point and was feeling pretty dazed. I went in the house, got my shower, got dressed and was thinking about the trip I still had to make to Chattanooga."

"Before I left, I'd went back out to bring our stuff in. In the process, I'd needed my phone for something or other and happened to glance at the screen. I saw where Renee had texted, asking me to go over and check on Brandon. Well, as I said, I'd seen his truck still sitting over at the house and thought that was strange for a Monday and knew he shouldn't have still been home but I was trying to finish getting the car unloaded. I was hustling to get ready to leave for Chattanooga when the phone started ringing again."

Regina: "I'd commented to Chris something must be wrong because Renee had been calling repeatedly. He was busy unloading our stuff so I answered his phone. Renee was upset and asked if one of us would go over and check on Brandon."

Renee: "I'd been texting, calling people all morning. Nobody was answering their damn phones. I finally got through to Chris and Regina and asked if they'd go over. Brandon and I'd talked the night before and he'd been in a bad way." Renee paused before adding quietly, "I was concerned because we had guns in the house."

Chris: "I was still taking stuff into the house so Regina went over to make sure everything was okay. I'll never forget what happened next-" Chris paused abruptly, emotion heavy in his voice. "I'd heard Regina screaming and immediately knew something was wrong." In a barely audible voice, he added, "It should have been me that went over there."

The gravity of the moment was not lost as heavy silence fell over the table.

Chris: "I knew about what was happening to Veterans but had no clue about the exact number. That number tears me up. We send these men off to war, trained to kill, then bring them home and expect them to turn all that off overnight? Expect them to come back and resume their regular, everyday lives? They're more than just numbers or statistics."

Renee: "I think there should be more in-depth classes about PTSD. Teach Veterans what might, what could happen and how to deal with it. They need to educate the families, something more than what they do now."

Chris: "I feel like we've turned our backs on our own. These are the guys who keep this country safe. We have to figure out something more to help them all."

Regina: "We didn't know anything about twenty-two before this happened with Brandon. I'd heard about the high suicide rates among Veterans but never saw any of that in him."

Jamy: "He'd called me over one time. Basically, he told me that he wasn't in a good frame of mind so I went straight over. He started talking about battle buddies who'd died in Afghanistan, how they'd all been getting shot at by insurgents. It scared me, but it was only that one time. I never thought to betray his trust and tell anybody about any of that. He trusted that confidence."

Chris: "I still can't believe it. Brandon had everything going for him, the whole world. At least I thought so. I was so proud of him for going back to school and getting his degree. He'd wanted to go back into the Marines as an officer." Chris paused as he took a slow drink from his bottle. "Brandon's loss has been one of the toughest things to work through. I've wondered a lot if there was anything I could've done."

Renee: "We didn't recognize any of the symptoms they tell you about until just before his death. Around us, he always had a smile or that goofy grin going on. Looking at things after the fact, we might have seen it coming. He had withdrawn from all his friends, wouldn't return calls, he wouldn't even talk to me about what was troubling him." Renee's voice softened as she added, "Looking back now, I think he must have had survivor's guilt."

Regina: "He'd have long breaks at work and would come over to the house and visit. He was going through some rough patches and I guess he didn't feel like being alone. That particular day started out as a regular morning. Chris was outside unloading our stuff and Renee had called to ask us to check on Brandon. I got to the top of the steps and-" Regina stopped mid-sentence.

Chris: "Talk about a state of shock."

Renee: "We're going to get through this. We all miss him."

Regina: "Brandon lit up the world. With him gone, it's just black. It still feels like the world has stopped turning."

Renee: "It's slowed down a lot, that's for sure."

Jamy: "I still expect him to call, like my phone is going to ring any minute and he'll be on the other end messing with me. He used to call all the time and leave stupid messages when he knew I couldn't answer. He'd pretend like he was somebody else."

Renee: "Oh my God. He used to do that to me all the time. He'd disguise his voice."

Jamy: "He'd do this thing where he'd call and start asking for donations-"

Renee: "Oh my God yes, yes. He caught me so many times. A few times he never fessed up, never told me it was him. Then it'd be a year later and he'd be all like, '*Mom, do you remember-*' and I'd be all, 'You did that? Oh my God.' There was one time he called me like that and I called him right back and asked, 'Was that you that just called?' and he was, '*Mom, what are you talking about?*' and I totally believed him. Well, he put Johnny Cosby up to doing it one time, and they called and told me that they'd just delivered twenty pizzas to my house. He said I'd ordered all these pizzas and they knew I was home but wouldn't answer them, so they were going to break down my door to get their money. I don't even eat pizza." Renee laughed. "I hung up on them. I called Brandon to ask if he had just called and of course, he said no. A long time after that though, he told me it had been him and Johnny."

Jamy: "Cole Wilson will have some great stories to tell. I wish you could talk with him face to face, or get all the guys together; the stories that would come out."

Renee: "I've had my days." Renee slowly sat back in her chair as she thought about her son. "I knew something was going on, but Brandon would say, 'I'm in a slump. I just want to be alone. I'm okay.' He wasn't.

Jamy: "He called me that time and I went right over. I guess he was reaching out. I'll never forget what he said. It made me speechless. The feeling that went through me at that moment, I mean it was that time, the only time he talked about him and his Marines getting shot at. Even then, he didn't seem comfortable talking about it."

Renee: "How do some people get through all that, come home, then go through the rest of their lives without feeling suicidal?"

-Roundtable II:
Birmingham, February 2016-

"I want the world to know how much he was loved and severely missed."

February 13, 2016, was a Saturday: the eve of St. Valentine's Day. It was another organized gathering of friends and family alike who had planned to congregate once again and celebrate the life of man known to and loved by them all. As guests began arriving, introductions were made, old friends acquainted with new. Familiar stories began being shared and inhibitions of not knowing what to expect that evening fell easily to the wayside.

Earlier that morning, a small group made a trip to a location situated not even ten miles away from the house. Their destination? Alabama National Cemetery, (ANC) the final resting place of a young Marine who would never know how significant his presence was in the lives of so many or how he had become the topic of a bittersweet story being prepared for the rest of the world to access.

ANC was also the place where the finality of an unwelcome reality had been thrust upon the lives of many unsuspecting people, a place where many had gathered and stood contemplating explanations to questions that would likely never be answered. Last but certainly not least, this particular National Cemetery was where scarcely three months previous, an author/Veteran and a Gold Star mother met for the first time to begin the process of putting together a tremendously difficult story that needed to be told.

What had been intended to be another series of 'one-on-one' interviews turned into an engaging round-table discussion about the young man who had determined to become a Marine. Everybody seated themselves around the dining room table in anticipation. Before they began, what was destined to become a traditional toast was raised to honor Brandon's memory.

When did you first meet Brandon?

Mitchel Sean Bunting, USMC: "We first met in school. I grew up in Trussville but transferred halfway through high school and ended up at Thompson (in Alabaster) my sophomore year. I can't put a finger on exactly when I first met Brandon, but he and I? We got along well. In my opinion, he'd seemed like quite the force to be reckoned with. Brandon was one of those guys known as 'King Stud on the Block.' The first thing I noticed about him was that he always seemed to be fighting and well, let me just say that nobody wanted to find themselves in a fight with him. "

Melynie Turnbough-Tapp: "I was 'Aunt Melbo.' I'm not related by blood, but his mom (Renee) and I have been lifelong friends. When I first met him, Brandon was just a baby, a squirt of like three or four years old. I remember him taking bubble baths when he was little." Melynie smiled as she remembered Brandon. "He was beautiful, a beautiful kid: always happy, always loving, and just wonderful. Brandon was an all-around great guy."

Samuel Langford, USN: "Brandon was always a jokester, and always had this charismatic aura about him. When we first met, we were both in grade school: first grade. My earliest memory goes back to when my family and I had moved into a townhouse in the area. Brandon and I must have been around seven or eight years old, and he lived three doors down. One morning, Brandon came to our door around eight-thirty to show me what I thought was an actual revolver/pistol. He started popping shots off and I instantly hit the deck; I mean face first, too. Turned out, it was just a cap gun. I got up, got dressed and we went out to play like nothing out of the ordinary had happened."

Amidst a background of laughter and miscellaneous chatter by multiple guests who had stopped by for the evening, the next question posed to the group at the table involved asking everybody for adjectives that could describe Brandon.

Without hesitating, **Mitch Bunting** immediately responded. "Passionate. Wait, is that an adjective?" Mitch paused briefly as he grinned. "Yes indeed: passionate. You know, some people would describe that more him being a bit of a hot head. I wouldn't call it that at all, I mean especially considering who Brandon was. He was a heartfelt, feeling, and compassionate man. I saw his way of handling things as an indication of the presence of passion. So many people these days lack that." Bunting was asked if there were any other qualities he'd describe Brandon with in addition to passionate. He sat back to think. After an exceptionally long pause, he rested with his initial choice of 'passionate.'

Sam: "Brandon was hilarious, witty, and short-tempered-"

Renee: (Brandon's Mom interjected.) "Brandon? Yes, short-tempered, sometimes."

Sam: "Passionate though, I agree. That's definitely the adjective I would use." Sam paused as he seemingly searched his thoughts. "Off the jump (from the get-go) our friendship evolved from his jokester personality. Brandon was the guy who was always cutting jokes, always making people laugh."

Melynie: "I can't describe just one thing about Brandon. To me, he was always my little 'Rooty-Tooty, Fresh and Fruity.' The greatest thing about him was that every time we'd meet or visit, regardless of when or where, it was always the same; 'Melbo!' I can still hear him now. It would be like no time had ever passed, every time. He was always so happy to see me." Melynie's eyes grew tearful as she shared her recollection. "Rooty was my boy. If any length of time happened to pass between visits, I'd be amazed when I'd see him and be all like, 'My God, Boy! What happened to you? You grew up!'"

Mitch: "While we were still in school, the Marine recruiters came out and thoroughly combed through the student body, trying to recruit all the able-bodies they could. It was funny because our school was more affiliated with Air Force ROTC but the Marines came in and cleaned house. Brandon and I joined at the same time but I went in about a month before him. We graduated high school May 25th and by June 1st was standing in the yellow footprints. Brandon had decided to go on our class trip to Mexico so he lost his slot. (I never got to go to Mexico.) My MOS ended up being 0811: field artillery." Mitch sat up a little straighter in his chair as he further explained. "In the Marines, every Marine is a rifleman first. No matter what your job or MOS, you're a rifleman first. We were trained in boot camp that if it came right down to it, we were to go out there and fight with the rest of them."

"When we came out of boot, we still had about six weeks of additional training to complete. I went MCT (Marine Combat Training) and Brandon went SOI (School of Infantry). If you aren't explicitly infantry, you go to one and not the other."

Mitch: "There are three phases to boot camp, so when I said Brandon came in a month after me, keep in mind, he was in Phase I while I was in Phase III: 'Crucible Phase.' So this one day as I was sitting in the mess hall eating, I was looking around at the other units. Now, you don't want to get caught doing that, but everybody does it. I was looking around and who do I see? Brandon Ladner. Sitting in there like that, you can't acknowledge anyone; drill sergeants are watching all around but Brandon and I gave each other the old 'Wassup?' nod." Mitch laughed in recollection.

Sam: When it came to sharing a story, Langford spoke quietly, as if deliberating whether or not to share his next statement. "I'm currently dealing with depression and my own PTSD issues, so I can relate to what Brandon was going through."

What was your initial reaction when you heard about Brandon?

Mitch: "I was in Panama City when I found out." He paused. "It was incredibly unfortunate. I don't know how to say this politically correctly but honestly, I wasn't surprised. It sucked. I don't mean to sound at all insensitive." It was obvious that Bunting was taking great care in selecting his next words. "It was something nobody expected but at the same time, I still wasn't surprised. I knew the things that plagued his mind, about a lot of the stressors he was experiencing but, you know, he was a great friend. 'No man left behind' you know that's what they always say."

Melynie: "I don't have just one special story, there are lots of them. I can't narrow them all down to one. It was his entire life," She paused, "-but my first reaction? I thought it was some sort of sick-ass joke. I was attending college at the time, was in class. I was crying and told one of my classmates (who happened to be a Veteran) what was going on. I was hysterical, couldn't believe it. It was no joke. It was so awful." Melynie composed herself. "You have to understand, Brandon had such a loving personality. There were times over the years that things had happened in his life, nothing this drastic but, he and I did talk. Sometimes things were pretty crazy in his life, but I never thought it was so bad. He never said he was unhappy or anything," Melynie paused, her eyes glistening. "-I wonder to this day."

Mitch: "When I first heard about Mission22, I didn't pay much attention to the organization. (Mission22 is collaboration between Elder Heart, a non-profit Veteran organization, and a global advertising agency. Elder Heart is comprised of former Delta and Special Forces operators who, because of their own personal battles with PTSD and TBI, have made it their mission to raise awareness of, enlist support for, and attempt to end Veteran suicide in America.) For me, that organization just fell to the wayside at first because there were already so many like it out there, but theirs is a noble cause, I don't think that," (long pause) "-let me just say that it's a wonderful organization and that especially after having the subject hit so close to home, I am fully 100% supportive of it."

Sam: "Aside from what Mission22 is about, all I have to say is this. As it is today, it's sad to say there's still no one specific resource for Veterans to get any help from, to help reduce any life circumstance that would disengage them from the symptoms they have. There isn't anything to pull them down off the level of severity causing these symptoms in the first place, symptoms causing so many to take their own life."

"Honestly, I feel twenty-two a day is a crock. It's such an arbitrary number. There's no concrete way to measure that logistic/data. For one, there's a lack of verifiable information. I know this first-hand as right now, I'm trying to expedite my own personal matter. The number is a great fallacy. It doesn't tell anything about what's going on with anybody because it can't." Sam paused deep in thought before speaking. "One is too many."

Melynie: "Twenty-two a day. Before this happened to Brandon, I had NO idea, had never heard that statistic. It breaks my heart. I knew PTSD existed, but until everything happened with Brandon, I had no clue it was as bad as it is. I knew military people have so much going on in their own ranks, but if you don't know, you don't know. More people need to be educated." Melynie took a deep breath before finishing her thought. "Brandon was the most amazing child and man that people will ever know. He was just amazing. I want the world to know that he was loved so much and that he is severely missed."

Sam: "We're all sitting here sharing our thoughts from different perspectives," He paused. "-relating to Brandon, my situation is different but it's the same." Sam seemed to deliberate whether or not to continue. "You asked about transition? Well, considering how I was essentially in limbo for six years with no transitional help whatsoever," he paused again "-when I got out, I had no opportunity to so much as see a doctor at the VA. The military operates by what they think is the right way to solve problems and they aren't open to any other suggestions or ideas. Nothing they've offered has helped me, but their rules are law and they won't bend."

"I mean, I guess they're doing what they can. It's hard to support that light at the end of the tunnel when every time you look, things are dark. It's taken a long time for my own situation to resolve but it's finally come full circle." Sam sat back and seemed to be studying the faces around him. "I've been in the same spot as Brandon, but for whatever reason, I didn't succeed with my attempt. The solution seemed a more peaceful resolution than working through all the stuff you go through. I've looked at what happened to Brandon and how it has affected people," Sam stood up and finished his interview. "-hopefully, people who choose to read Brandon's story will see how this issue hasn't gone away. It's still here, an ongoing problem."

Mitch: "You know, if I were interviewing myself, I'd' have to ask me the following question. I would ask, 'Self, what would you say to Brandon right now if you could talk to him?' Mitch sat back and crossed his arms. There was no trace of humor in his voice as he continued. "This may sound horrible, but I'd call him an asshole. I'd be all like, 'Hey Bro, why'd you pop smoke before the mission was fucking complete?' but then again, I also understand. I get it: completely."

"People can sit back and analyze the shit out of this and preach or comment about how he left this life, that he was selfish or how it was a permanent solution to just a temporary problem, but you know something? When it comes to PTSD, especially combat PTSD, what ordinary people don't know is that this shit affects you for life. When you are going through it, it doesn't feel at all temporary. Every night when you go to bed, you dive right back into the same scene. That's your center, your dreams. You go back every fucking night to combat. It happens to me." Bunting paused. "Every night. No, I know I'm not fighting or at war, but I'm still there in my thoughts: that in and of itself is hard to deal with. The Marines train you to kill efficiently and you come out knowing how

to be a warrior and how to use all the instruments of war. You don't come out ready for a nice little job on the outside."

"Like it or not, people don't have control over everything in their lives. For the majority though, at least when they go to bed at night, they can escape the everyday hassles. For a lot of Veterans, it doesn't happen like that. I wish I could say to Brandon, 'Come on, really?' but at the same time, I'd tell him, 'I love you, Bro' and let him know I got it. It was a decision, a decision he felt he had to make." Mitch leaned back in his chair. "I don't know, I guess I think that PTSD keeps a person from leading a full life. Every Veteran knows going in that it's a possibility when they come back. Long for short, I'd give Brandon a huge hug, pop him on the back and tell him 'everything's gonna be okay.' I feel he found his peace. We'll all eventually heal from this, but it doesn't make anything better. It's so true, 'War is hell.' No matter who tries saying anything different. War is so awful. It's the worst thing you could wish on any human being. To go back to that every single night and have nowhere to run?"

"Sleep is supposed to be that 'comfortable' place you go to escape the rat race. Instead of comfort, a lot of vets end up going back to the awful places, potentially for the rest of their lives. It's terrible to think you can be handicapped by that. It's very debilitating. I'm glad Brandon's story is being put together because it's going to provide awareness and exposure of a huge issue." Mitch paused as he took a slow drink from the glass in his hand. "I would talk to Brandon. I wish I'd been here. Although it wasn't acceptable, I can see why he did it. I honestly wasn't blindsided or surprised that it happened. Like I said, Brandon was an extremely passionate guy and passion is passion. When you experience those emotions, you can go from zero to a hundred in a heartbeat. There are no shades of gray. Everybody deals with shit differently but when somebody you know well goes out the way Brandon did, it's tremendous. No one will ever be the same again. 'Bro, I love you, man. You're my Devil Dog. We've been through some shit. It's just not fair, but in the end, I guess fair doesn't matter."

Before the decision to write about this Marine's life came about, before any roundtable discussions were held or flag presentations set up, there first came the news of his passing. The idea of talking with all the people who knew him came when the idea for the book came along but long before any of that happened, there first came the aftershock of the news of Ladner's passing. To give the world a better idea about whom exactly Brandon Ladner was to so many, it was only natural to wander through pages he had posted on that popular social media network that we all know about and read through the various things he had shared for the rest of the world to see. Aside from the many pictures of family and friends, there were other things there as well that offered a glimpse into the life that he led.

The love Brandon had for his friends was as clear as picture after picture revealed a happy, smiling, bear of a man who always seemed to be having a good time. Sprinkled among all the photos of family, friends and fellow brother Marines were occasional thoughts shared by Brandon that though probably not done intentionally, revealed another side. He seemed wistful, almost as if there was something missing in his life.

Brandon shared the following quote by Ronald Reagan:
"Some people go their whole life wondering if they made a difference. Marines don't have that problem."

And then, there was this:
"You can only hide emotions for so long."
"It seems like the civilian life is so slow. I'm ready for something to happen, maybe a civilian deployment out to California..."
"The greatest times are never remembered..."

In addition to revealing another side of Brandon, the power of social networking proved how quickly news could spread as well. It never takes long for anybody well-connected to touch base on or comment on the latest 'hot topic of the day'. The same can be said for shocking matters and unexpected news. When word got out about what had happened to Brandon, the internet exploded and became a source of instant confirmation for many.

"I served with Brandon, in the summer of 2009 in Nawa, Afghanistan with Alpha Company. I fondly remember your son. My most vivid memory of him comes from the end of July during evening chow. He'd sing random Tom Petty songs, and if anyone knew the name of the song, he'd give us extra chow."
Brandon was a great man, and I am so sorry your family

*is going through this right now. Sgt. Ladner was my brother
and continues to be. For that reason, I ask for the location of
his final resting place so that I may pay my respects. Again,
I'm deeply sorry for your loss, I pray that God gives you the
strength and fortitude to continue pushing forward, and lastly,
I hope you know that your son was an amazing man."*
   Semper Fi   Make Peace or Die

Renee responded in kind:

*"I'm looking forward to meeting two of my son's Marine
brothers. They're coming in tomorrow from out of state tonight to pay
their respects. I feel so much love and support from everyone that ever met
my son, and there are still hundreds of people that I don't know. Thank
you all from the bottom of my heart.*

*Brandon never met a stranger, he was always eager to shake
hands and gain another friend. He was such a fun, happy, loving person
and always had a good joke or just a huge smile to let you know how
everything was going to be ok.*

*I remember a couple of years ago I was riding with Brandon and
some car passed us and he honked the horn. I asked 'Who was that,
son?' and he replied, 'I don't know, but she sure was pretty.' I just
smiled and said, 'That's my boy!' He was so full of life and so motivated
to reach his goals. I never realized how much he struggled with PTSD.*

*I'd like to ask each and every one of you to write and call your
local senators, representatives, and push for Veteran stability packages,
bills to help fast track and treat those with PTSD. The numbers are
astonishing!"*

There were hundreds of other posts from that day: disbelief
expressed by scores of people all across the country. The questions,
the devastation and inevitable grief that followed in the wake of
Brandon Ladner's death hit the airwaves en masse. Twenty years
ago, finding out about what happened wouldn't have been so
instantaneous. (Twenty years ago, the news still wouldn't have been
any easier to acknowledge, either.) Instead of struggling with the
logistical nightmare of attempting to contact and gain permission
from so many different writers who had expressed their thoughts
and condolences after Brandon's death, interviews were collected
instead.

☐

-Cole Wilson, USMC-

"Nobody will ever compare to Brandon. He was a real stand-up guy, always smiling, always making people laugh."

"The first time Brandon Ladner and I met, we were on a bus leaving Camp Lejeune. I can't remember where exactly we were going, but it was right after boot camp. I think this was near the end of 2006. A mutual friend introduced us, I remember him telling me, 'You've got to meet somebody. You'll love him' and ole Brandon and I hit it off right away. Within the first five minutes, I knew I wanted to see what this guy was all about. He became my best friend. It's crazy because we never spent a day apart after that."

"His sister Nicole (who was in the Air Force) had been stationed in Hawaii at the time he and I were finishing our own training in the Marines. When it came time for Brandon and I to fill out our paperwork to pick where we wanted to go, he was like, *'Dude, we've got to fill out the same duty stations'* so we both picked Hawaii, California, and Lejeune.

I don't know how long it was, but we finally got our orders for what duty stations we were going to. Brandon got California and I got North Carolina. Of course, never one to be discouraged, Brandon came up to me the next day and told me how he'd found somebody who'd been assigned to California. He wanted to talk to our First Sergeant and see if we could switch assignments with this guy. I thought Brandon was crazy. 'They're never going to let us do that,' but Brandon talked to him anyway and told him about the situation. Never in a million years did I think we were going to get to change our orders but guess what? We both ended up being sent to California with the First Division, Fifth Marines (1/5). I don't know how he managed it, but somehow with his charm and

Brandon just being Brandon, he did it. That's kind of how every day was with Brandon. *Every* day was awesome."

When Cole Wilson was asked to give several adjectives that would typify exactly who Brandon was, he only paused briefly before sounding off. "Confident, self-assured, humorous, friendly, enthusiastic, ambitious, and extremely sociable. Brandon was a straight-forward kind of guy and probably the funniest person I've ever met in my life. He was always on the go, always wanted to be around people and always doing something."

"He was so outgoing. Everywhere we went, he was always the life of the party. No matter where we'd go or who we were around, he always made friends. It was crazy the effect he had on people and how he could get anybody to open up. Everybody always wanted to be around him. I've never known anybody else like him. Nobody will ever compare. Brandon was a real stand-up guy, always smiling, always making people happy."

Cole laughed before continuing. "He'd kill me for telling this one. When we moved into our apartment in Oceanside, California, we ended up having female neighbors; there were two or three of them over there. The way things were set up, their kitchen window looked right into our kitchen window. Well one day, Brandon comes out of the bathroom completely naked. He had his bits and pieces tucked between his legs and was standing there just inside the kitchen asking, '*Tucked or untucked?*' Of course, I'm dying laughing. He happens to look across from the kitchen window and suddenly goes, '*Oh shit!*' then runs through the doorway, stubbing his toe, I mean almost to the point of crying. He turned around and said to me, '*Dude, those girls were all standing there looking at me and laughing.*'"

What were your first thoughts when you learned the news of Brandon's death?

"First thoughts," Wilson echoed the question and inhaled audibly before responding. "Brandon had texted me that night but I'd already gone to bed. When I woke up the next morning, I'd received a text that said, '*I'm sorry Wilson. I love you. I'm sorry. Tell everyone else I'm sorry.*' Then a little later, I'd received another text that said, '*As you were. I'm good.*' So I texted back and asked him what was up. I mean, I'd seen where he had texted back 'As you were. I'm good' so I'd figured everything was fine. Later that same day, I was at work when around ten o'clock I received a call from an Alabama number that I didn't know. I got this eerie feeling. I didn't know who it was either, so I didn't answer. The caller left a voice mail. It turned out to be Brandon's brother-in-law's brother. Of course, I was a little curious as to why he, of all people, would be calling me. The message he'd left didn't seem so bad, but it still seemed a little odd he'd called. I stepped outside, called right back and asked what was up. That's when I found out. I literally dropped the phone."

"I'm not a crier by any means. I mean, I haven't cried since I was young, but at that moment, I was in absolute shock. When I processed what had happened, I just couldn't believe it and cried my heart out. It didn't make any sense to me: didn't seem real. I didn't know what I was supposed to think because I had just talked to Brandon the day before about a new lifting routine that he was going to be starting. I immediately dialed his number and of course, he didn't answer. It was so unreal. The next thing I did was get in touch with his mom, Renee. When I finally got through to her, she was hysterical. It was really happening. To be honest with you, it was the worst day of my life. I've never felt so empty."

Cole grew silent as he gathered his thoughts. With emotion heavy in his voice, he slowly continued. "It was the worst day of my entire fucking life. I wish I could've been more there for him. I mean, I knew he'd been feeling down and out. He'd told me as much. See, the way things worked between me and Brandon was if we didn't talk every other day, there was at least a text message. I mean, we stayed in touch even after we got out of the Corps all the way up to the night he died. He'd told me he was having relationship issues at the time, was stressing some about school, work, and money: stuff we *all* stress about. I told him, 'I've been there, too.' I'd just had a bad night and had told him all about that. We talked for a couple of hours. 'I'm here for you. You've got a bunch of people here for you.' He cheered up and sounded better, so I thought everything was fine." Cole paused as he collected his thoughts. "At the time, Brandon was working at the VA a few hours a week at the same time he was going to school. He was helping direct people where to go, like what services they could use or who to talk to and stuff like that, so I told him to go to the VA. Everything would be ok."

"He was down and out for a few weeks, but out of the blue, I received a text from him that said, '*Dude. I'm clear.*' He was back to cracking jokes, just like the old Brandon. That lasted a little while but then, from out of nowhere, it happened. I feel like I failed him, that I should've reached out to more people to let them know he was depressed but I took his word that he was feeling better. I saw the change in his attitude. I mean, he and I had been together for four years, 24/7. You get to know a person when you're with them constantly like that. We may not have been blood brothers, but we were brothers for sure. I've never been closer to anybody in my life than I was with Brandon Ladner. It still doesn't seem real. I miss that guy more than anything. I'd give anything to change things."

"Twenty-two a day: obviously, with the 1/5 situation (an unusually high number of suicide-related deaths from one particular deployment) and the number of other brothers we'd all lost to the same thing, I already knew a lot about that number. I think it's completely unacceptable. The VA, *somebody* should be doing a lot more to bring that number down. I don't know how, or who can do anything but it's something that needs to be addressed. It's hitting too close to home. I've lost too many brothers. There's got to be something that can be done. It's sad, heartbreaking, especially since it has hit so close to home."

"For me, I can tell you transition was hard. I feel like I'm still in transition. When you become a Marine, you get so used to a set routine for however many years you are in then one day, you EAS and your military life is over. Brandon and I went to this three-day-long seminar class-like thing that taught us how to write resumes and take interviews, but," Wilson paused. "-I applied for so many jobs after 2010 and never heard anything from any one of them. I held several jobs after I left the military, applied to places that were supposedly 'Veteran friendly' but blah, blah, blah. I think it was all a crock of shit. Companies might hire a few Veterans for tax purposes but that's about it. I've talked to so many people who've experienced the same thing. I'm still trying to transition," Cole paused again "-I start the police academy next month. Hopefully, things are finally going to turn around for me."

"Brandon and I both hated the fact that we got out of the Marines. Things seemed so much simpler when we were together. (He'd wanted me to move to Alabama.) I wish they'd done more for our transition. The way I've looked at things, we should've had jobs lined up before we ever left the Corps but there was no way to look for jobs on the outside while we were still on active duty. I can guarantee that both Brandon and I would've stayed in had we known the way things were going to work out."

"Once we left the military and got back to the real world, we felt like we were just random Joe Schmoes, particularly after coming out of such a tight-knit organization as the Marines. I'm sure it's like this for a lot of guys. Join the military, do your duty, get your DD214 then go back to living in your parent's basement and working some minimum wage job: from Superman to nobody in 2.0. It sucks. Talk about culture shock, and it happened so fast. I wish they would have done more, they've *got* to do more." Cole paused. "As for me and Brandon, when we got out, we were both like, "Okay. What the fuck are we supposed to do now? I still want to be a Marine. What did we just do?""

Following Brandon's death, Cole posted the following… (Reprinted by permission.)

> *There are so many things I want to say to you brother. I'm sitting here in my smoking spot looking at my phone wanting to call and talk to you about how shitty these past few days have been. I'm truly going to miss our nightly conversations. We've been best friends for eight years, lived together for four and probably spent a total of six months beating the shit out of one another just because we're both stubborn, fucking jarheads. We spent two deployments together. We were just two kids, scared to death but we had each other's back from day one. Things always seemed to work out when we were together, it was usually a shit show but it worked out. We always seemed to find a way to get through all the bullshit.*

> *I just keep hoping I'm gonna get a call and I'm gonna hear "Wilson…." and you're gonna tell me it will all be okay, we will figure a way to get through this. My heart just hurts for you bro. I'm devastated to know you were hurting that bad. The bond we had is something that will never break and I will cherish it always. There's so many 'B-lad and Wilson' stories that can be told but we both know about 75% of those are way too explicit for Facebook. To say you were a best friend is a complete understatement. I wish I could have been there for you bro. To tell you it's all gonna be okay and were*

gonna get through this like always. I love you Brandon I will never forget you and the times we had and the impact you had on my life. It was an honor to serve with you and an even bigger honor to call you my friend. Until we meet again. Semper Fi brother! I love you.

☐

-Denise Kiel-

"He was the guy who always liked to have fun."

"The first time I ever met Brandon was when he and my son Cole (Wilson) were still stateside. Cole never seemed to have his phone on him, so whenever I needed to talk to him about something or other, I'd have to get a hold of him through Brandon. It was so adorable, too because every time I'd call, there'd come this sweet southern voice on the line. Brandon, always polite was like, 'Yes ma'am, no ma'am.' Every time."

"I used to travel all over the United States and on one occasion, I was able to go out and visit Brandon and Cole in California. Even though I'd never met Brandon face-to-face to that point, after having talked to him so many times on the phone, I felt like I already knew him. The first thing that struck me about him was his smile, and how his blue eyes just sparkled. I remember sitting there watching those two interact. They would drink their beer, laugh and joke around and act just like a couple of kids. I was so content sitting there just watching them."

"I took them to lunch and after we were through, I happened to ask if they had any beer left at the apartment. They both sort of hung their heads and answered, '*No*' so I offered to buy them some. They lifted their heads up and were like, '*Really?*' So off we went to restock their supply. We went to this huge liquor store out there in California, and the two of them went running around like kids in a candy store, going through, picking up this, that, and the other."

"We ended up back at their apartment and started watching the movie '*The Hangover.*' Sitting with the two of them, I ended up laughing my ass off. You have to understand, they'd already watched this movie at least half a dozen times before I got out there. I don't know what was funnier, watching the movie or watching those two. Brandon and Cole were out of control that night. They were so funny together. Those types of friendships don't come along very often. When they do, you cherish it." Denise paused before continuing, her voice softening. "You know, you don't see guys having a deep friendship like that, where they call and talk to each other two and three times a day. The two of them had something special."

How did you learn about what happened to Brandon?

"I happened to have the day off from work and had been in town having lunch with my mother and sisters. I'd turned my phone off, but for one reason or another, I happened to check my messages. I saw where I'd received a call from Cole. I remember thinking how it had been odd for him to have called so I called back. He didn't answer so I left a message and told him I'd call again in a little while. That time, when I called back, he answered. I could tell immediately something was wrong. 'I really need you to come over here.'"

"Cole lived on the other side of town from where we were having lunch so I flew over there. All these things running through my head and I wondered what could have possibly happened. All of the sudden, it hit me; something must have happened to Brandon. I came squealing into Cole's driveway and rushed through the door. There was my son, sitting in the corner of his garage smoking a cigarette, holding his head in his hands. He looked up at me, sobbing. That's when he told me; Brandon had killed himself. I couldn't believe it. Cole was an absolute mess. I'd never seen him like that. It was horrible."

"As far as Brandon's funeral went, I'd told Cole we would do whatever it took to get him to Alabama. Folks here in town were amazing. I mean, what they did here," Denise paused. "-there's a gentleman in town who works with this group that does all kinds of things for Veterans and long story short, that group paid for Cole's ticket to get down there. There was no way he was NOT going to go."

What adjectives would you use to describe Brandon?

After giving the question a lot of thought, Denise responded. "Brandon was a character for sure. He was a loyal friend and to me, you could tell just by the way he acted was that he was also a gentleman. He had one heck of a sense of humor, too. That kid cracked me up. Just seeing him and Cole together was great. I got so much enjoyment out of watching those two do what best friends do together. They were so funny, and to hear Brandon speak? I could sit and listen to his voice all day long. I loved his accent. He had such a great smile. He was a very handsome young man."

"Renee and I always laughed because I'd call the two of them 'my boys' and she called Cole her 'son from another mother.' Cole loves Brandon's mother dearly, and I think it's so sweet how she adores Cole."

"As far as naming just one outstanding quality about Brandon, I can't. There wasn't just one thing about him. I will say this though: a total stranger would have no problem identifying who Brandon was in a room full of people. He'd be the guy standing there with a great big beautiful smile on his face making everybody laugh. Brandon was the guy who always liked having fun."

"This is just a matter of opinion, of course, but I think Brandon was a lot more sensitive than anybody ever thought or gave him credit for. I mean, just thinking of all the things this war exposed them to, all the things they had to do and endure, I think Brandon was more sensitive than maybe even he knew about himself. For all those guys, when push came to shove, you had to learn things about yourself that you never knew. I think when he came back, some of the things he saw or experienced might have been things he never came to terms with."

"Brandon had been going to the VA. That was the thing; when he was a student in college, he had changed majors because he wanted to change how things were being handled at that level in the Veteran's Administration. He had so much life to live and so much to offer. There isn't a single day that goes by where I can wrap my head around the fact that it happened. I look at all his pictures, his face, and think about all the great things he could have done."

"Brandon had such a sweet, soft side to him. He wasn't just a big, tough Marine. That's what they train them to be, how they train them to act but that's not who he was. He was an excellent Marine,

don't get me wrong, but deep inside, I don't think Brandon ever completely lost who he really was."

"Twenty-two a day: I'd heard about Mission22 and knew what they were all about but until it happened to my son's best friend, I never focused on it. Of course, I thought it was horrible, sure but it means a heck of a lot more to me now. It makes me sick. ONE is one too many as far as I am concerned. Something has to be done. We're so willing to send our people over there but when they come home, all we can muster is a 'thanks a lot, now go home' and maybe a pat on the back. Society as a whole doesn't do enough, they just abandon them. I feel we need to be more involved, especially after they come back."

"Reintegrate these guys, develop a better transition process. They go off to fight, do what they have to do but when they come back home, they're changed. They don't want to be in crowds or ride in cars, or, I mean, I know for my own son that leaving the military was hard. They need to teach them to be civilians again. Human beings can only be put through so much. I don't care how they think they've been conditioned."□

Valentin Rascon, USMC-

"I would say that he was a true leader, a fine example of a Marine."

"Brandon Ladner was an amazing Marine. We first met in March of 2010 when we were both in the 62-Area with the 5th Marines at Camp Pendleton in California."

"Brandon was many things. He was always a gentleman but he was a lot more than that. Ladner was brave, loyal, charming, intelligent, loving and welcoming just to name just a few adjectives. One of his more outstanding qualities though, was how he genuinely cared for and about the men serving with him. He took good care of his troops, always working with them. I mean, for example, if a group of Marines working or building on something, Brandon was right beside them doing the same work. He never allowed other superiors to take advantage of his troops or over-work them, either."

"I had to travel an hour and a half to work, and was having to deal with some personal issues that resulted in me having a lot of appointments I had to keep and did a lot of driving back and forth. Brandon always allowed me to do what I had to do. He understood things that were going on and did what he could to help make things better. I would say that he was a true leader, a fine example."

"I couldn't believe it when I heard the news of his passing. I still can't comprehend it to this day and still have a hard time with it. You know, I found out pretty much by accident. He had already finished his time in the Marines, and I was getting out and he and I were supposed to meet up, go hunting or fishing or something. So I was on Facebook and was looking for him when I found a post by

Cole Wilson. Then I found Brandon's Facebook account and requested him as a friend. That's when I started reading all of these 'Rest in Peace" messages. That's how I found out. I found him, but I was a little late."

"Transition for me, I am still dealing with things. I'm at the VA right now taking classes for PTSD, I've been homeless, I've been a lot of different things. It's been hard, but I'm doing okay. I'm learning new things and hoping to be able to give back and help others who are experiencing issues and struggling as I have."

"I'm dealing with the recent loss of another Marine I knew. The best way we can honor all of those who sacrificed so much is to give back to those who continue to serve. 'Leave no man behind.' I want Brandon to be remembered as the hero that he was to everybody he ever came in contact with. He inspired us all to be better; to do better, to think better, to expect better. I think of him every day. He loved this country with all of his heart. He made me a better Marine, taught me how to better prepare for promotions, he even showed me how to be a better leader myself for my younger Marines. I feel like I was a better person, a better Marine because Brandon Ladner inspired that in me."

-Luc Dyer, USMC-

"Brandon was the most energetic people-person in a room."

"I met Brandon Ladner sometime in May of 2009. We'd went to country and got a string of attachments. Brandon was an attachment to my squad during our deployment to Afghanistan."

"Adjectives I'd use to describe Ladner? I only knew him from a Marine perspective, but he was a fun, exciting, energetic, outgoing, clean-cut, muscular, and extremely friendly guy."

Luc Dyer was asked to describe an identifying quality about Brandon that could be used to pinpoint him in a room full of people. "Oh wow. Brandon was usually the most energetic people-person in the room. He was the type of guy who didn't wait to be introduced to anybody or have to be told what to do. He was always anticipating what needed to be done. Brandon was the guy always surrounded by people and if not, he would surround himself with them. He was the exact opposite of a loner. He was always involved in something."

"I remember when we first met at Camp Leatherneck. Leatherneck was a staging area for troops coming into Afghanistan. When we got our attachments, it happened to be on a non-training day. At that point, we weren't due to ship out for another month. Here comes Brandon. He came over with a few other guys, and already, he stood out. He was just a corporal at the time. 'I'm Cpl. Ladner and we're attached to your squad. We're a few tents down. Do you want us to move closer?' I told him we didn't have anything going on and to just show up at 0600 for PT. He didn't leave. Instead, he offered to hang and acclimate, learn the ropes. He was like that new guy on his first day at a new job. At that moment, we didn't need him for anything but he was persistent in wanting to hang out and just be there. We had nothing to do."

"Well, I'm an early person. I've never liked people waiting on me so I was up at 0430 to start getting ready for my day. At 0500, I looked out at this bench and there was Cpl. Ladner already waiting, an hour ahead of time, waiting for his first training day, all geared up. That image of him defined him that entire deployment. It was funny and I was like, 'Who is that guy?' You could always count on Brandon being early."

"I found out about Brandon's death on Facebook. Someone had posted on a group page asking who had information on Ladner. During the same time frame, there had already been a history of eight or nine other Marines who had taken their lives from the same 2009 deployment. The suicide rate had reached a point where it was getting out of control. I wondered what in the world was going on when I saw all those posts. It blew my mind. Here was another guy we'd served with, you don't imagine a guy like Brandon feeling a certain way, certainly not the type who would take his own life. I never saw that one coming. I'm sure many others were just as surprised."

"I think Ladner's suicide started this push with the 1/5 guys with bonding. His suicide compelled us all to start our own network, encouraged us all to get back to being more the family like we were when we served. Twenty-two a day. I work with Project22 raising awareness for those twenty-two Veterans a day. That's a powerful number."

"I must admit, as far as the entire transition process goes, I'm an outlier. My transition was simple. I was lucky to be in the right place at the right time. Mine was a well thought-out process and involved a lot of preparation on my end which made things much easier. I took appropriate steps that set me up for success. The prep and work in the front end had positive dividends in the end. I refused to get out until I had a college degree. I had three years of non-deployable duty stations to help me decompress. I think each person is different. I had a good cool down period. I was home a lot with family, was able to complete my school, got set up with the appropriate people, and it worked out well for me."

"A Marine goes into the service at the age of 18. His deployment generally sees him get out at age twenty-two. Combat is all he knows. Transition gives a Marine the resources he'll need, the tools necessary to transition back to civilian life but he doesn't know how to use them. In his mind, he's still that eighteen-year-old who joined the Marines and is not at all prepared to go back to the life he left four years previous."

After finding out about Brandon, Mr. Dyer sent the following to Brandon's mother Renee:

> *You don't know me, but I was your son's squad leader while he was attached to A Company 1/5 in Afghanistan. I just found out about Brandon and am so sorry to hear. The numbers from 1/5 are growing too high. I am heartbroken. Your son was a great Marine. He always stayed up late to make sure we ate and he never complained. He loved going out on patrols with my guys and I always welcomed him. I wrote a book about that deployment entitled 'A Battle Won by Handshakes: The Story of A Co 1/5.' Your son is mentioned in my book and I feel I should send you a signed copy. It isn't much but what he, and we did is now forever written."* □

-Michael Rivera, USMC-

"If I could only get all my guys to remember the days when they had each other's backs, that they carried each other, they needed each other..."

"I first met Brandon when I checked into the First Battalion, Fifth Marines I think around the end of 2007. He was part of their motor transportation section and he was just a lance corporal at the time. An adjective that immediately comes to my mind when I think about him is 'knucklehead.' You have to understand though, in the Marines, any PFC (private first class) or lance corporal can be classified as a knucklehead. These are the young, energetic guys who like to joke around; a lot. At work, they're constantly trying to make each other laugh. It's just what they do, like office mischief sort of stuff. One is okay but when there's a room full of them, things get crazy. They're always trying to work the system in some way or another, figure the easiest way out." Rivera paused briefly. "Brandon's partner in crime was Cole Wilson. Every time I'd see those two together, I knew something was up."

"I didn't work close with Brandon, but the one thing I know about him, especially individuals like him and Wilson, is that when it was 'go' time, when a mission needed completion, they were on top of things. I'll say that about all my Marines, but I knew those two especially were big Marines you could count on. If anything needed to get kicked around, I'm sure they were the ones doing the kicking. Wilson and Ladner complimented one another and that was the worst part about it all. They were like Frick and Frack."

"Back on base, I'd have to go to each section to check and see what everybody was doing for the day. I could always count on catching those two with their hands in the cookie jar, so to speak.

Theirs was a true brotherhood, I mean just like brothers. There was no question about either one of them taking a bullet for the other. They pushed each other when needed and I'm sure that went on all the time."

"When I first learned of Ladner's death, my first thoughts were, 'I've lost another one.' Brandon wasn't the first Marine we lost like that in the 1/5. Of course, I started thinking 'How can I stop this? How can I reinvent the wheel? How do I get them all back to the days when we were out on patrols together?' I'd give anything to have that ability to still keep them close. We were doing patrols around the forward operation base (FOB), and Brandon was one of those guys that no matter what, even at 0300 in the morning, he was the first guy grabbing his ruck and weapons and getting ready to go over the wire. If I could get all my guys to remember the days when they had each other's backs, that they carried each other, they needed each other..." Rivera's voice trailed into silence. "I'm all like, 'I know you miss it, guys. Get back to those days and realize how much you, as individuals are needed' but I can't get them there."

"Brandon was a great guy, a great kid. I mean what a great kid to have, had you seen him, any of them in action, you'd have been in awe. He seemed to have everything going for him, too. After he got out of the Corps, I'd hit him up on Facebook quite often and he looked like he had all his shit together. Then suddenly, that all seemed to disappear. His was a huge loss, not only for his family but also for us. He was that good of a Marine. I can't change what happened to Brandon, I want to so much, but I can't and I am watching as this sort of thing is continuously happening. It's not a good feeling to watch somebody fall and feel you have no control in allowing things to get that far."

"PTSD is a whole different war. I've experienced it myself. Sure, they give you resources, they'll give you drugs, but nothing seems to help. It never goes away, not completely. You've just got to deal with it. PTSD has to evolve and grow with you." Rivera gathered his thoughts. "At first, when I returned home from combat, my family paid the price. By the time my daughter noticed and spoke to me about it, I didn't like what I heard but she was right. That's when I went for assistance. I still struggle with it every day, every minute. You know about the (Justin) Swanson incident. I relive that every day. I smell it. I see it. I've had many instances like that happen around me but that's the one that bothers me most. It should have been me. I'm sure there are plenty of guys out there saying the same thing. We did everything right that day, but as far as the whole PTSD thing? I don't know how to tell my guys to live with it. There's nothing else that keeps me going."

"How do I feel about twenty-two a day? We've got to change it. Something has to happen. If you say twenty-two a day, 365 a year, that's a huge number. Twenty-two × 365, that's over 8,000 souls. Imagine if I had that number: frontline individuals like no kidding, they're outside the wire, and they were all good at what they did while they were in-country. If I could bottle that up, whatever 'it' is and go back in time and give it to these Marines, I would. These guys were at their best when they were running and gunning, but when they came back home, America didn't give them what they deserved. 'You were in the military. Big deal.' Well yeah, it kind of was a big deal. You got kids who enlisted in the Marines immediately after high school; they went out for three or four deployments during the course of their enlistment and then, 'Boom!' It's all over. When they get out of the Corps at the age of twenty-two, that's all they know. What do they do now?"

"Transition," Rivera echoed simply. "-mine was hard. I left the Corps with a bad taste in my mouth. I mean, I understand rules of engagement, but they weren't working at the point when I was still active. Then, to have to transition back home? When I came back from Fallujah, it was one of the worst experiences I've been through. If my wife wasn't there for me, I'm positive that I could've become a statistic. I wanted to go back, I wanted that adrenaline rush. Coming home, I didn't have any of that, but America didn't care. What can you do about that? Then I saw the light. I admitted I had PTSD. You hide it. When you wake up in the morning, you put on your face, but when you're alone, that's when the demons come out. It's a struggle."

"Transition is hard. You have to force yourself to go out and find hobbies, some kind of group, support; something. There are all kinds of VA support groups out there. I try to bring any Marine in the neighborhood that I know over to the house. I mean, why not? 'Come on over and have a beer ' but these young guys? They don't want to suck it up and involve themselves in the VFW or Legion scene. 'That's for the old guys.' No, it's not. They have to find a niche, something but to them, it's like admitting a weakness, a vulnerability."

"When I was in the Corps, I was a leader. From my point of view, I needed EVERY guy in a fight. If these guys could realize that the fight isn't over, that they all have to come together and that it's okay to seek each other out, I think this whole PTSD thing would be more manageable. They won't let themselves do that though. If anything I say or share can keep somebody from pulling the trigger, I'll do it! Write it out! Share it! Hell yes! Once these guys start talking, they'll open up. You know those drunken calls at 0400 in the morning? I get many of those. 'Gunny you got a minute?' You're damn right I've got a fuckin' minute. It may be 0400 in the morning, but I got a minute. I have guys on the edge right now, some guys I can't find. 'Have you heard from this guy? Do you have so-and-sos number? Get at me.' We're out, but it isn't over, but too many don't want to acknowledge that."

"You have to reach out. I don't care what company they were with: alpha, bravo, weapons or whatever. They had a big mission and they did it well. Why are they faltering now? 'You're a Marine, tougher than nails. Hang the fuck in there, until your last breath, until your weapon is empty and dry.' Marines live by this, they WANT to do that, they want to be the Dan Daily's, the Audie Murphy's and Chesty Puller's but then they lose all that when they come home. The military hasn't got its' hands around it yet on how to make successful transitions happen. Right now, at discharge you might get one or two classes, and then you're out: good to go. 'Thanks for your service. Here's your DD214. Bye.' We've got to change that. 'Leave no man behind' are words to live by."

☐

-David McCreary, USMC-

"You got this. Don't worry."

"It was after Labor Day, and we'd just left Okinawa (Japan). I was checking in with the 1/5 (First Division, Fifth Marines) at Pendleton back in California. After checking in and getting out of my service Alphas (uniform), I got to go meet my guys. I was a sergeant and had just left a unit in Okinawa where I was the head guy over thirty Marines. I mean, mine was the word of God. Cali (California) was completely different. There was already a lead sergeant established and I became just some secondary guy with no real responsibilities. I expected to go in there with that 'hard-charging' sergeant' thing going on but quickly realized the guys in Cali weren't new boots. These Marines had already been in for a while and were more laid back. I only had ten, maybe eleven Marines to take care of. That's when I met Brandon."

"I was all like, 'Let's train these guys on how to work' and they were all like, 'What? No. We just go in and do the stuff we're told.' Within two weeks we became a small group of Marines who'd gotten close. When it came down to first impression of Brandon, he was always one of those people out front. He wasn't waiting for you to introduce yourself to him; he'd introduce himself to you first."

"Brandon didn't seem to have a serious bone in his body, but when it came time to flip the switch and be serious, he did it. He had that kind of laugh that you could hear from across the warehouse. He'd talk about things and just make everybody laugh. He never had a problem speaking to anybody. A general would walk in, and Brandon'd be the first person to pop up and say, *"Hey sir, how's it going?"* He'd get a wild hair and somehow would convince you to go along with whatever he had planned on doing. He operated without any fear. I didn't get to see him much in Afghanistan but I can tell you that he was courageous, always loyal to his friends. He'd have your back in a minute. He was more like a brother. We could get in a fight but if anybody else got in, we knew who had us. If you were down, he'd try to make you laugh. If you were up, he was right there with you trying to make you laugh even more."

"When I first find out what happened to Brandon, I was in college just sitting outside of class. I'd come in about half an hour early and was just sitting there studying, checking out some things on Facebook and then I saw where somebody had posted about Brandon. It was like getting kicked in the chest by a horse. I thought, 'No fucking way.' The first person I called was Cole Wilson. I could hear it in his voice." McCreary paused, taking a deep breath before continuing. "That was a short conversation. I told Wilson, 'Call me if you need me' and went looking for my professor. I was walking down a hall full of nineteen-year-olds and mind you, I was thirty at the time so I felt I couldn't let myself cry. The last thing I wanted to do was walk down that hall, but I had to. I couldn't stay at school. I called Cassie (my wife) and told her what was up then got in my truck and kind of lost it for a little while."

"Cassie and I started going through a list of who we needed to call to tell about Brandon. I wanted to tell my guys personally, not have them find out about it on Facebook. I had a hard time keeping everything together. My Marines had spread out all across the country when they EAS'd (discharged). I finally got off the phone and walked into the house. Everybody could see by the look on my face that something was wrong. I told them what happened to Brandon and they were all caught off guard. It was such an unexpected pause in our lives, one we had no control over, like being stabbed in the gut with somebody slowly twisting the knife. I'd called Cassie and told her to get home. "Nothing else matters right now." I met her at the car. Cassie was just as close to my Marines as the rest of us were with one another. She was like just another one of the guys. The next few days were hard. "We have to go to Alabama."

"Twenty-two a day; I wouldn't say that I knew the exact number of Veteran suicides but I knew it was high, I knew this guy and I'd known that guy or I'd see somebody's name from the 1/5 but couldn't place all of them. I didn't want to get on Facebook and see the fact that we had lost another one. Over the past two or three years, I didn't know it had gotten as bad as it had."

"There are a few stories I can share. I've been thinking about this and want to shine a good light on him. Brandon was that guy, it was his last weekend and we were all talking about getting together. We were going to meet at one bar in particular, close it down, then go back on base, get past the gate and go back to my house. At the time, Cassie and I had two children; one was just six weeks old and the other was two years old. My parents were at the house for a visit and to see me off for our next deployment."

"Well, around three-thirty in the morning, my youngest needed a bottle. You have to understand, all of us had gotten together for one big night before we had to leave so we were all hanging out downstairs. My dad came down to make the bottle and walks in on the bunch of us drinking and still having fun. Brandon was the first one to introduce himself and was all kinds of concerned. (He was the type of guy that even if you'd only known him for a short time, he could make you laugh so hard.) Brandon was worried that we'd been too loud and raising too much ruckus. 'We're sorry sir. Did we wake you up? We are so sorry.' My dad's response? "I'm just making a bottle.""

"We were getting ready to go on our last leave block before deployment. Brandon, Cole, and one other guy weren't there and nobody could get a hold of them. We were about to have to report them UA (unauthorized absence) when Cole finally called. I asked where they were. 'We partied too hard last night. The gate guard called the MPs.' As it turned out, they had flipped their car but everybody was okay and they didn't get into any trouble for being UA. Everyone was just thankful they were all okay."

"Then, there was the time we were getting ready for deployment and Brandon asked, 'Hey, do you remember when we wrecked that car? The night before that, I got two tickets up in Orange County. Should I take care of those?' I told him, 'Seven months out of country and getting a bench warrant? Yes, you need to take care of those.' He was all like, 'I've never been to court. What do I do?' So I had to guide him through the process.

I picked him up the next morning and he was squared away, looking like he was going on liberty. I'd told him he needed to take a copy of his orders for Afghanistan to court but he didn't have them. I figured he had no chance in hell but he goes before the judge with this parade rest and speaking respectfully but being very loud about the whole deal. Of course, the judge asked for his orders. '*I don't have them.*' The judge just said, '*Come back tomorrow.*'"

"Brandon always had that 'Don't worry about it' thing going on. I told him to dress nice, be respectful, etc. Brandon comes out in worn and holy jeans, frayed on each leg. 'That's what you're going to court in?' I asked. '*The judge likes me!*' he declared. I sat there thinking about how this judge only knew Brandon for like all of three minutes and I was all worried, 'You were speeding and Cole flipped a cigarette out the window.' The judge ended up dismissing everything. Despite the fact Brandon had returned for court in the rattiest pair of jeans he owned, that judge still let him off."

"We were at Twenty-Nine Palms, three weeks in the desert at Camp Wilson. Our cell phones only worked in weird places out there and we barely had running water for showers. So there we were, suffering and sweating and freezing in the desert, and we had to prep for the Warrior Dinner. When it was all over and done, we also had all the mess to clean. The grunts had been cleaning everything and in the process had clogged the disposal. This ungodly mess started coming up through the drains in the floor. We ended up having a room full of water with all this mess in it and so we spent the rest of the night cleaning up. Sometime around five or six the next morning, there were ten of us with the key to this one Gunny's office. He'd been a real dick all night long, so we went into his office to chill and started talking trash about him. His cordless phone was sitting on the desk, so Brandon took it and put it between his butt cheeks. 'He'll appreciate this.' I couldn't believe he did that. Later, Brandon called the Gunny."

"Transition. After my first enlistment, I was like, 'Let's do thirty years' but I had to EAS after only eight and a half: medically retired. Things were a little shaky for me. I didn't have any direction. If I'd stayed in, I'd have had to go admin and be non-deployable. I got home and didn't know what to do. For me, it was like 'wake up and find something.' A post office job eventually came up. Long story short, it was a hard transition."

"Once I got a job and back into school, things were still tricky. I had nothing in common with any of the kids that I had to deal with at college. And even my job at the post office was tough at first. I worked at the window or did admin stuff but it was difficult dealing with civilians: just very hard. You get out and lose that military cadence; the cadence of regular life is so different. I miss the military routine. You serve your country, get out and then it's like you get dropped into the middle of nowhere."

"It took me awhile," McCreary paused deep in thought. "-and I hid these things from my family. It's still difficult. I wanted to go all the way, make first sergeant but now I'm like, 'So is this my end game? Is this what I'm supposed to be doing?' I was good at the military. I suppose I'll figure it out. Talking with my brothers helps alleviate things. We've got each other's six. I think communicating with fellow service members is key. Don't get me wrong, my family has been great and amazingly supportive but just when I think I've made a step forward, I think "Damn it! Shit!" There are things that just creep up sometimes. I can call another vet and we can share common experiences. We make time and get each other."

"I was able to get on the 1/5 Life Line to get some things off my chest and let everyone know I was fine. I can't spend the rest of my life worrying about this shit. I've got to find my feet. The fact that that I'm a Marine, well I just don't want to talk to somebody I don't know and portray that persona. I can talk to other Marines and they see it, they get me. So many of them are going through the same shit. I have actual people I can talk to. I have bonds with fellow Marines, guys who've been there and have seen me at my most vulnerable. I know that I have a support system, but there are others though who don't. They need to know that shit's gonna blow over. 'You got this. Don't worry. It's all there.'"

☐

-Cassie McCreary-

"I don't think anybody knows what's going on. PTSD: a lot of people out there have no way of knowing what these guys have been through."

"I first met Brandon in September of 2008. My husband had been stationed in Okinawa for three years and we'd just come back stateside and checked in with the 1/5 at Camp Pendleton. It took me about a month to get to know the Marines under his command. Brandon and Wilson were the first ones I met."

"The first night they came to the house to hang out, Brandon drank nothing but dirty martinis. One of my girls loved green olives, so while Brandon was making all his martinis, he was also feeding my daughter olives on the side," Cassie laughed and added, "-that diaper change was awful. (He got on-line later and ordered a bottle of just the olive juice for the next time)."

Are there any particular adjectives you'd use to describe Brandon?

"Adjectives? How about 'life-of-the-party'? Is that an adjective? You just always knew when he was around. Brandon would be the life of the party. I never knew him to meet a stranger. He'd talk to everybody. Let me tell you a story. I remember right before they were deployed for one particular tour, our little group went out clubbing. We came home and everybody was so tired but Brandon and I made it to like three that morning. My in-laws had been over to watch my girls while we'd all went out and around that time, three o'clock, my father-in-law came downstairs to make a bottle for my daughter. Brandon just started talking to him and was all like, *"We didn't wake you up did we?"*

"We've been trying to think of different stories to share but there's just so many. Let me tell you this one. Brandon and Cole had already EAS'd. They'd been gone for about a year and my husband David was missing them. So as we bought Cole a plane ticket to surprise David for his birthday. We'd told Brandon and his wife about the surprise and everything but little did I know that the two of them had been planning a surprise of their own. Cole, David and I were all hanging out at the house and this taxi pulls up. "Are you expecting anybody?" It was Brandon and Ashley! They got out of the cab and all of us spent the entire weekend partying."

"PTSD. It gets hard sometimes for me because I see what my husband still has with his Marines. Brandon was special to me, too. I'm good friends with these guys but I don't have that Marine bond like they have with one another. They stay in touch, too. All anybody has to say to any of the others is 'I need you' and they'll drop everything to be there."

"When I found out about Brandon, I was still in school working at my internship. David texted me, 'Call me right fucking now!' I looked at the text and started wondering, "Oh Lord. What happened?" He called and told me about Brandon and I just went into shock. "No! I don't believe you. Proof, I need proof." He assured me, "Cassie. This is real." And we went back and forth. "I don't believe you." Then I went to Facebook and saw all the posts. I started crying. I didn't know what else to do."

"Twenty-two is a lot. As for people on the outside, I'm not sure if that number means anything unless they're connected to it somehow. I don't think anybody knows what's going on. PTSD: a lot of people out there have no way of knowing what these guys have been through. It's ignorance."

"Let me tell you about our transition period. I prepared myself before David came home. He'd planned on being a lifer. We loved the lifestyle. I mean, I loved every person I met, but then David got shot in Afghanistan. Making that transition was hard for both of us. I had to make the transition right along with him. Our neighbors in the Corps had become my family, too. I told my husband, "We're gonna get through this." He sort of eased himself back into civilian life. We still have some struggles. Marines have that ego thing going on. They're told, 'Be the best' 'You're the baddest, most fearless-' and then to have to send them back home? To what?"

"In the Corps, my husband David was a staff sergeant. He was somebody who had a number of Marines under him, was in charge of weapons and patrols. He went from leading Marines to selling stamps at a window. Some nights in his sleep, he still struggles. I try to ease him back. Sometimes he'll talk about it, sometimes he won't. I'm super proud of him for how far he has come. That part is never going to go away. He isn't ever not going to miss that part of his life. Brandon Ladner was certainly a large part of that."

☐

-Millard Downey, USA-

"He was one of the strongest people I know."

"I met Brandon Ladner when we were in fifth grade at Riverchase Middle School. We became good friends while playing football. My dad happened to be the coach and Brandon and his stepbrother Beau both played. Turned out, Brandon also rode dirt bike as did I so that was another thing we had in common. We started riding together and grew to be close friends."

"Brandon was spontaneous, a little bit goofy and an undeniably funny guy. He was loyal, for sure. He'd do things for others without expecting anything in return. To be such a big, brick shithouse of a human being, he cared so much. His circle of people was well protected. I mean, I know that he'd do anything in his power to protect me, I have no doubt.

"Brandon always had a way of lightening any kind of situation that there was. I could be having a terrible day, go talk to Brandon for a little while and he'd turn the whole situation around. I mean, the floor buzzed around him. The way he carried himself, people were just drawn to him. He got along with everybody. That's the best I can put it. I can't explain why or how but Brandon was just that kind of guy.

"Here's one story that kind of stands out. There was this one bar that we used to out drinking at all the time. One night Brandon and I decided to go out and we ended up drinking pretty hard. Brandon came up to me and was all like, *'Man, I'm starving. We need some food.'* So we ended up driving to McDonald's and buying about twelve double cheeseburgers, mowed them down then returned to the bar, back to doing our thing. Mind you, this bar had a small parking lot and when we went back, it was full of cars so we ended up parking out back. We went in and stayed another two or three hours before Brandon was like, '*I'm ready to go.*' We walked out to the parking lot and ended up searching for his car for about 45 minutes. He actually called the police because he thought somebody had stolen it. We ended up walking out behind the bar and suddenly he was all, '*You're not going to believe this shit. I found my car.*'"

"How did I find out the news about Brandon? It was a little after seven in the morning when Chris Espey called and asked me what I was doing. I knew something was wrong just by the tone in his voice. He told me Brandon had killed himself. Well, I knew a couple of different Brandon's but for some reason I knew exactly who he was talking about. It broke my heart. I'd just woke up but was immediately confused. I mean, anytime Brandon ever had any problems, he'd call. Brandon was my 'go-to' guy. We'd been through a lot of the same stuff together. Losing him was like losing a family member."

"I got off the phone with Chris and sat there a second staring at the wall, thinking it was all a dream. It took another two or three phone calls from other people for it all to sink in. I called his phone, hoping he'd answer. Obviously, that didn't happen."

"I wouldn't have wanted to find out about something like this on social media. I'm more into personally connecting with people and think this entire social media craze is draining society. I mean, I don't know. Twenty-two a day is mind-blowing. How is it that so many people a day can get to that low of a point in their lives and feel that's their only option? It breaks my heart that there's so many of my brothers and sisters in the military who feel they've run out of options. To have that much pain, to have that much built up inside of you to the point that you can't talk to a regular civilian and expect them to understand? To find out that Brandon had done that and had never called me was hard for me to understand. I think he just made up his mind and that was it. I think saying that he 'popped smoke before the mission was accomplished' is accurate. I never thought Brandon would be one of those people."

"He was always so strong. I knew he was carrying around a lot of survivor's guilt. It may make me sound selfish but if a guy like Brandon could do this, where does that put me? He was one of the strongest people I know. I was mad, sad, and confused to think that he just kind of gave up. I wanted so much to be able to talk to him, to tell him we'd get through it together."

"Transition out of the military was rough for me. I mean, it was *really* rough. I had a lot of problems when I got out: still trying to chase that adrenaline rush you get in combat. I was self-destructive. I'd been a medic in the infantry and for years was thinking, 'I survived this: what can hurt me?' I've only recently gotten to a point where I've finally accepted a lot of things that went on. It took a lot."

"The biggest thing that helped me was having people like Brandon who I could talk to. The VA can pump you up with all kinds of therapies and drugs, sure but my best tool was my support system. I still struggle at times, but I've found little ways to occupy my mind and to cope so that I don't slip into that depression."

-Jonathan Echeverry, USMC-
"The world lost a good person when Brandon left us."

"I think the first time I officially met Brandon Ladner was a little into the start of our deployment. It was around the summer of 2009 He was working over in the mess hall, and we were over there helping out," Echeverry paused. "-Man, that seems like such a long time ago."

"What words would I use to describe him? Brandon was a lively guy. He wasn't shy; was always relaxed, always had a smile and was always joking around. He was just a very happy guy who had an infectious smile, the kind that automatically made you feel at ease. Working in the mess hall, we had to be up before everybody else. So in the mornings, he'd get up and always had this great attitude. It seemed like nothing could ever bring him down."

"We were hanging out one time with another friend who was a radio operator. This guy was already friends with Ladner before I'd met him but those two were always freestyling (spontaneous rapping). They'd be together rhyming tight and be all funny doing it. It was actually intriguing considering the environment we were in but it was also pretty neat. I learned to never judge a book by its cover. Brandon was a regular Marine version of M&M."

"I was shocked when I found out about Brandon's death. It was the most unexpected thing. It never crossed my mind that Ladner was somebody who'd take that path. He was so confident, good looking, had a great attitude; from the outside, anybody would assume he was having a good spot in life. I mean, you wouldn't assume he'd be the guy to have those kinds of demons. It was just all so crazy. I thought it was some kind of mistake, but no, it was exactly how it was told. It was sad; unbelievable."

"I've felt so many random things since I've been out. I mean, don't get me wrong. I'm a pretty high volume kind of guy. I'm happy but some of the emotions I've had this past year alone have just about overwhelmed me. I feel like I understand some of the things Ladner might have been going through. There's always something, a void you can't fill no matter how hard or what you try. Twenty-two is a horrible number to think about. It could hit anybody. One second you are completely happy and content and the next is like a switch somebody has flipped. You don't know what's happened or what you are about to have to work through."

"The first few months after I was discharged, I stayed home for the most part. I got done with my deployment and came home but had to take things slow. The first year went by and I found that I liked it best when I was working with prior service people. There was this one guy I worked with who was prior service and we got along well. It felt good to be working alongside him, but then he left and I had to compensate for that feeling."

"I buried myself in a lot of work. I wanted to be working all the time because there was something; I mean I felt like I was alone. I was focused on my family, my kid and my wife but sometimes, like during my commute to work, it felt as if I were waiting for something. It was like all this anger would just well up inside me. I wouldn't outlet it or anything but it was there, and this overwhelming sadness."

"Brandon and I used to go out on patrols together and we'd talk and just share things. He was a great guy, an outstanding individual. He was awesome. During chow and stuff, we'd talk and pass the time. Brandon was a good guy to be around." Jonathan paused. "The world lost a good person when he left us."

"The people I feel the worst for are his parents and family. The people who were closest to him have to feel his loss on a daily basis. They're the ones with the heavy burden. They wake up every day and realize that he's gone and that's so sad. Those people have to bear that day in and day out. That has to be tough. Brandon had such a huge presence."

☐

-Dean Gustafson, USMC-

"Brandon hasn't been the only friend I've lost to PTSD. Ladner was an incredible Marine and a great friend and brother of mine. I still think about him and everything he went through to fight for us all. RIP to my friend and brother. Semper Fi"

The first question asked of everybody for this book project was of course, 'How did you meet Brandon?" Fellow Marine Dean Gustafson laughed a little before revealing how he and his brother Marine met. "When did I first meet Ladner? That's a good question. Actually, the first two Marines I met in fleet were Brandon and Cole Wilson. We were all over in San Mateo at Pendleton in the mess hall. I was a brand new Marine, what they call a 'boot.' I was all kinds of nervous but remember Brandon telling me not to worry. 'The higher ups already know you don't know what you're doing anyway, so no worries.'"

"Brandon Ladner was a very strong-willed and intelligent guy. He was so motivated and fun to be around, and had such a big heart. Brandon cared about his fellow Marines. I mean, he genuinely cared for all the people he served with." Mr. Gustafson paused before quietly adding, "I miss him. I miss talking to him."

When asked to pick one outstanding quality to describe Brandon, Gustafson didn't answer immediately. After giving the matter some thought, he responded, "I don't know that I could pick just one. Brandon was caring. He had a tough exterior but once you got to know him, and he knew you, he'd give you the shirt off his back. He was a very caring and empathetic kind of guy. There isn't just one word that could describe him."

"I had an apartment in California where he used to come over and drink and watch football games with everybody, or we'd all go out bar hopping and have a good time. He'd have house parties at his place, too. Brandon was just fun to hang out with and be around. There isn't just one story to tell about him, either."

"There is one thing I'd like to share that I think kind of speaks about his PTSD. There was an incident one time when we went out and Brandon and some guy got into a dispute about the number of deployments Brandon had been on. They got into a bit of an altercation. Back then, I didn't know a whole lot about PTSD but I look back at things now and can say when we were out doing our thing, I can say I saw the signs. At the time, I was like, 'Gosh just let it go. You know what you did Brandon' but for Brandon, that was a hot topic. He was proud of being a Marine and of his service to this country."

"I couldn't believe when I found out about Brandon. I was devastated, literally devastated. I have other friends in the Corps who've lost their lives to PTSD and those were all tragic of course, but Brandon's death really bothered me. It messed me up for a little while. I'd have moments at work; I just couldn't believe it had happened. It was surreal in a lot of ways. I wish he would have said something. I was mixed between feeling this tremendous sadness and anger. I've thought long and hard about it and feel like I saw the signs and wonder now if I could have done more. I lost a good friend to PTSD. I wish he would have said something to me."

"The number twenty-two is a tragic one. It's unacceptable. I'm familiar with the suicide rates, especially in the Corps. I feel it is completely unacceptable. Better care and more resources need to be made available for so many vets. It's obvious that many need them, the resources. I don't know what resources Brandon had in Alabama but I wish he could have taken advantage of them. Not enough is being done right now, and as far as my own transition? In a lot of ways, I'm scared. I got out and immediately used my GI Bill so my transition was okay, but I'm scared because of the number of Veterans who are so vulnerable to PTSD. As I said, Brandon wasn't the only friend I've lost to PTSD."

☐

-Michael Goodson, USMC-

"I don't want to remember the end of his life. I want to remember all the good times."

"I first met Brandon on the USS Tarawa when we were both working in the galley. He was Funny, hilarious, always smiling, always happy. He was the type of guy that you always knew was in the room. There was quite an age difference between us but as it turned out, we had some of the same background. I think that's why we meshed so well. It seemed kind of peculiar at first because, at the time, I was thirty and Brandon was twenty but he was a little beyond his years. He didn't act like any ordinary twenty-year-old I'd ever known."

"I don't know if anybody else has told you this about him yet, but one thing I admired a lot about him was how he could rap. I mean, he could flow. They call it freestylin' and Brandon was amazing at it. In the galleys at night, we'd be trying to freestyle but here'd come Brandon. He was so good at it. I remember we'd all went out on the catwalk in Australia one night and I'd taken video of him doing this. The bad news though, is that I lost the SD card and now I don't have any of the pictures or videos of our time there. I consider Brandon one of the closest and best friends I've ever had in my entire life and I think about him every day. I hope something good comes from this (his book)."

"Everybody called him 'B-Lad.' When Brandon EAS'd (discharged) from the Marines and went back home to Alabama, it wasn't long at all before he was saying how he regretted getting out. We were both finishing up college and used to talk about it quite a bit. We'd had the time of our lives out in Cali. He loved California and wanted to get back out there so bad. Brandon loved the brotherhood, loved being a Marine. This was a guy who was the best person to hang out with, just an amazing person."

"I knew he was going through a little bit of stuff because we confided in each other. We'd talk for three or four hours at a time about life, our plans. I was having a lot of issues myself and hadn't talked to him for almost a year, but he knew what I was going through. I'd sunk pretty low and was embarrassed about so many things going on in my life. I found out we'd lost him about a month after he passed. I went back on that social media and saw that he'd messaged me a few times but I'd never responded. That shook me. I regret so much that I wasn't there to talk to him when he needed someone to confide in."

"I don't want to focus on the end of his life; I want to remember the good times. I'm glad someone is telling his story He was such an unbelievable guy." Mr. Goodson added, "I have to say, what you have named the book, it's perfect. I've ridden motorcycles my whole life, too. Let me tell you a story. I had a nice Harley waiting for me when we got back from deployment, I mean a really nice ride. When we got back, me, Brandon and another guy all went out to Oceanside to Brandon's place. Both of them said they could ride a motorcycle. The first guy gets on and as it turned out he couldn't ride. Brandon was all like, 'Let me on.'

"So there we all were, out there on the beach. Brandon was just in sandals and a swimsuit but he took off on my bike. I have to admit, I was pretty impressed. He could ride but the other guy? Not so much. Brandon loved motorcycles and that became part of our friendship. It was great, and like I said, he could really ride!"

When asked how he initially felt when he found out about Brandon, there was an instant silence. After taking a moment to think, Mr. Goodson responded softly. "I immediately felt bad because I wasn't there for him. He was a brother who knew my darkest secrets; I wasn't there to be his buddy to unload on. I know he had to have been feeling a lot of pain to do that. I regret not being there for him."

"Brotherhood; we believed in brotherhood in the truest sense of the word." Mr. Goodson drew a deep breath. "I think I speak for a lot of people when I say this. When we came back, we were expecting something, like feeling the same sense of belonging that we had with our brothers. As far as I know or have experienced, not many people ever find it again in the civilian world."

"I was not at all familiar with the whole 'twenty-two a day' statistic about Veteran suicide, but I know enough now to recognize that it's not a good thing."

"Transition is different for everyone. Mine's been tough. I'm still a work in progress, every day. I fall off the path every once in a while, but the only thing I can do is utilize my resources. I have to work at it. Everything is different and I've finally realized that. I've had to evolve with the times and keep going. I think if Brandon could have changed things, he'd have kept going, too. I think of him and I work a little harder on my own life; to keep on keeping on. The transition was tough but as far as now, I'm the best I've been for a while. I have a wife, two kids; I have people I can depend on and trust."

"You'd think with how far we've evolved with everything related to war that we'd have come up with something to keep this from happening to the extent that it has. I didn't go through all the same things Brandon did and can only imagine some of what he saw when boots were on the ground. A lot of guys don't feel like they can reach out. Brandon had this big personality; he loved life so much but it got him. If it could get to a guy like him, it could get any one of us."

"I miss him every day. I look forward to this book coming out and finding out things I might not have known about him. He loved the Marines. His story might help somebody else out there who's having a rough time."

-Ashley Seal-

"You never get over something like this. You just have to learn to get through."

"I first met Brandon when I was sixteen back when we both worked at Food World, a local grocery store. He was a bagger and I was a cashier. My best friend was the one who'd had a crush on him first, but Brandon and I ended up dating. We'd gone to school together but had never met until we ended up working at Food World. It was funny, too because our first date was at Mr. Bob Lipsey's (Brandon's step-father) house. Bob used to be my neighbor. When I walked in the door, he was thrilled to find out Brandon and I were dating."

"One of the many outstanding qualities about Brandon would be his entire personality. He wasn't just good looking and sweet," Ashley laughed at the comment she had just shared. "He also had this great personality. To describe Brandon to a stranger, I'd tell them how he was so full of life. He was always the life of the party, always happy, and could make anybody laugh." After a brief pause, Ashley took a breath and continued. "Brandon was just, well, he was kind. I never met anybody who didn't like him: anybody. He always had such an upbeat spirit. Let me put it this way; there was never a dull moment when Brandon was around."

"I have to think about this a minute. There are so many stories I could share. I know a lot of inappropriate ones but I probably shouldn't share any of those. He was a character for sure, a real character." Ashley paused again as she searched her thoughts. "Brandon loved surprising people. While he was in the Marines, there were several times he told us he couldn't make it home on leave but he'd show up, surprising everybody."

"I spent ten years of my life with him, I mean, we were married. It's hard to think of just one special memory. One of my favorites though, happened when he was still in boot camp. We were writing and calling back and forth, talking all the time. That's when he ended up asking me to marry him. We married in Alabama then moved to California. That's one of my favorite memories."

"When I first found out what had happened, I was in absolute disbelief. There was no possible way that something like that could happen to a man like Brandon. He cared so much about what other people thought of him. Other people's opinions mattered. That's why it seemed so crazy that he would ever take his own life. It just wasn't in Brandon's character."

"I'd woke up already in a bad mood that day to begin with, but I was sitting in my mom's house when Renee called. I'll never forget it. I was in an instant state of shock. My heart crumbled into a million pieces. Brandon was the last person in the world I thought would ever do something like that." Ashley's voice caught as she continued speaking. "I walked out the back door and told my parents the news. About twenty minutes after that, I drove over to Renee's. I still couldn't believe it. I used to think about what I would do if anything ever happened to Brandon. What would I do? Brandon had always been there for me, even after we divorced. My worst fear came true the day he died."

"Twenty-two a day. Before Brandon, I never knew anything about that number or what it meant. Chris Espey told me a little about it, but after Brandon died, this whole experience made me want to learn more. It made me hope to God that maybe we could do something to prevent more of this from happening. That number is insane."

"While we were married, Brandon and I had our ups and downs but we still loved each other so much. He always had so much going on what with college, working at the post office and the VA," Ashley paused. "-and I say this next thing out of love, but you know, Brandon was a real Mama's boy. He absolutely loved his mom Renee, would talk to her several times a day as a matter of fact. Brandon didn't go a single day without talking to her, ever."

"My life has changed. It was the most tragic thing. Brandon was my soul mate. Life didn't exist to me without him. Despite our circumstances, I'd still have done anything for him." Ashley paused, carefully choosing her next words. "Things have gotten better as far as coping. After his death, I thought I'd never be okay again. People don't understand that and it's hard to explain. It's taken some time.

I used to make myself miserable every single day. I mean, I used to cry so much more."

"Brandon was my best friend. Losing him changed my life. I wouldn't wish this feeling on anybody. A lot of people can't understand that. You never get over something like this. You just learn to get through it. Brandon had so many friends and he touched everybody's lives. I guess there's that, at least we all have each other. I couldn't move forward until I was ready. I've slowly learned to cope, but that's all. I miss him. I loved him so much, and always will."

☐

-Michael Linder, USAF-

"Brandon Ladner would have your back no matter what the situation."

"I first met Brandon Ladner in High School during freshmen year. I'm unsure of the actual event that led us to start talking with one another, but I seem to remember one story in particular where we bonded and began hanging out together. I want to say we were in Earth Science class and as usual, most of us were taking an opportunity to catch a quick nap in class. One of our mutual friends, who was also sitting in the back row, was taking his nap time quite seriously. Brandon and I were sitting back there, and in typical Brandon fashion, he whispered, "Watch this!" as he let out the loudest fart. I mean, it echoed off the chair he was sitting in. He quickly directed the blame to our oblivious sleeping friend. Brandon's confidence led no one to question that it had been Brandon and not our friend who'd done the deed. The entire class busted out laughing. It was quite hilarious at the time and from my best recollection, was one of the first things that got us talking."

"One adjective that immediately comes to mind when I think of Brandon is the word honest. He'd always tell you exactly how things were and never sugar-coated anything. He was trustworthy as well. Brandon Ladner would have your back no matter what the situation. He was the very definition of a friend. Whenever I'd have a bad day, I could always count on meeting up with Brandon, beer in hand, ready to talk about the issue."

"One of the best qualities about Brandon was how he enjoyed being around other people. He enjoyed the kind of impromptu get-togethers that usually involved a campfire and a couple of brews. He never took issue with meeting new people and would often invite them along as if they were family. Brandon was an amazing host. I've never seen a man get as excited as he did whenever he had an opportunity to cook for friends and family. When we all got together, Brandon would make dirty martinis, which tended to be extra dirty."

"The most memorable story I have about Brandon happened when I was just joining the military. Brandon had already completed his enlistment in the Marines. He played a big factor in me determining to raise my own hand and take the Oath. Unlike Brandon who had joined the Marines, I went into the Air Force instead. He was there for me every step of the way, answering every question I had. Although I'd joined the Air Force, he was okay with that. He'd always tell me how jealous he was of my joining the Air Force, condescendingly of course. He'd reference the Marine dress blues and "making panties drop."

"The day I left for basic training, Ladner was there. He met me at the recruiting station and stayed until I got on that bus. He even followed the bus for a couple of miles, giving me a salute before driving off. That was the type of person Brandon was. He was true and genuine, a rare friend to have. He wouldn't steer his friends in any direction that he wouldn't personally put himself or stand shoulder to shoulder with you in."

"It's tough to tell just one story about Brandon, because we had so many. Most of them revolved around life, military, and our future endeavors. What made most of the stories between us was his love of my car. Every time he came into town, he'd always call and ask to just go ride around town. Although every time that happened, it always led to him driving me around. What made it peculiar was the fact that I didn't trust just anyone with my car. I had a 2003 Ford Mustang Cobra which was pretty powerful but for whatever reason, I trusted Brandon behind the wheel. I'd let him drive us around for hours bar hopping or just talking. Before he'd start driving, I'd tell him to be careful. His typical response would be, "On our friendship... P!" It was a done deal. Once that 'P' was dropped, it was a bond as strong as a brotherhood."

"On nights we didn't drive around, we'd visit and share a brew or two together. When we'd go our separate ways at the end of the night, I'd have to rev that engine loud enough so Brandon could hear it. One cold night after we'd not seen each other for a year or so, we met for a couple of beers. After we'd finished our visit and I was about to leave, we made a deal. He wanted to hear the Mustangs engine one good time. So as I pulled out onto the four-lane, I accidentally let it get a little crazy and lost control of my car. I hopped a median, crossed three lanes of traffic and was facing the wrong way in the blink of an eye."

"I quickly recovered and pulled into the nearest parking lot. Here came Brandon, pulling in right behind to check on me. Although no major damage was done, I believe we both grew up that night. (If I remember correctly, from there on, I just revved the engine instead of acting all young and dumb. Brandon accepted that token of gratitude.)"

"When I first found out what happened, I'd been on deployment. I'd just gotten off shift when I received a message. *Did you hear what happened to B-Lad?*" I immediately broke down and felt so empty. I didn't know what to do, especially being so far away at that moment. I found one of my good friends and told her the news. She was able to get me to reminisce about all the good times and truly made that moment easier. It still upsets me though, how he was so genuinely proud of me for serving in the military but that I was unable to be there for him when he needed it most."

"I believe the 'twenty-two a day' statistic is twenty-two too many. It's sad that we have men and women putting their lives on hold for something greater, so selflessly serving this country only to return home and not receive the respect and care they deserve. Something as simple as a basic phone call to check up would be a better feeling. As an active duty member myself, I know that we'd like to know our leaders care. We don't want to feel expendable as some of them tend to do. Each of us left home, our lives for a specific purpose. We didn't enlist in the military just to have that sense of purpose obliterated or our dreams shot down by people believing we were dime a dozen pawns. We went far and wide for our country. How is it that our country can't do the same for us?"

"As mentioned, I'm currently on active duty but I plan on separating once I've completed six years of service. I've deployed twice in two years and don't want to continue this pattern. I respect every man and woman whom I've served with but I believe it's time for me to punch my ticket. I'll always carry my service to country with me just as Brandon did and will wear it proudly on my sleeve. (Maybe re-enlist later?) My transition process won't be an easy one, but I believe Brandon wouldn't have guided me in the wrong direction. He helped me get to where I am today, and I'm grateful for him. Brandon was a true brother. I promised him when I got back home, the first round would be on me!"

☐

-Alex Kenner, USAF-
"He taught us all some serious life lessons."

Many people that Brandon Ladner surrounded himself with were those themselves influenced by the path Brandon had taken into the military. Alex Kenner was no exception. The evening Mr. Kenner gave his interview for this project found him stationed in Nevada, still serving on active duty in the United States Air Force.

"Brandon and I met during homeroom of our ninth grade year at Thompson Middle School. We were assigned seating according to alphabetical order. That was how we ended up sitting near each other; all of us were into riding dirt bikes at that time, trail riding. It was a great experience. Brandon was a nice guy."

"How would I describe Brandon Ladner? He was always fun to be around and accepting, but I'd also have to say that he was a little intimidating for his age. Brandon was talkative, approachable, and just an all-round nice guy. If there were just one particular quality I'd share, I'd have to say it would be his loyalty. Another friend and I had both decided to join the military and we'd always try taking leave at the same time so we could visit with one another back home. I swear, *every* single time we went home, not an hour would go buy before Brandon would call and say, *'Let's go out for a beer.'* Even though we all had left for the military, he stayed in contact." Mr. Kenner paused before continuing. "It was because of Brandon I joined the military in the first place. I wouldn't be the man I am today if it hadn't been for him."

"One thing you've probably heard about Brandon was how good he was at freestyling. (Rap music.) Every single time we'd be chillin' at Ms. Renee's or like at my going away party before I left for basic training, we'd get a little drunk and just start freestyling. Brandon could do it like nobody else."

"We were at the 'Black Market' a club in Birmingham, chillin' outside. It was just Brandon and me. We were out on the patio area at the bar and happened to witness some guy getting tased by the police. Brandon was so funny. He started imitating the guy." Alex paused in thought. "It became a running joke. No matter where we'd be, Brandon would just call out, "Don't tase me, bro.""

When asked what his first thoughts were when he found out about what happened to Brandon, the question was met with silence. Kenner finally answered. "Honestly? I didn't know what to think. At first, it was almost surreal. People post stupid things on line so I wasn't sure what to think. I was stationed out in Las Vegas at the time. I'm not much of an Internet kind of guy but by the time I'd found out anything, well, I remember Mike Linder asking me if I'd heard about Brandon. Mike explained everything."

"I remember that day like it was yesterday. I was in uniform and that was probably the first time I ever cried in all my adult life. If I'd known what was going on in his mind, I'd have requested leave in a heartbeat and tried to be there for him. I started thinking and wondering about if there was anything I could have done to prevent it." Kenner drew a deep breath. "Brandon Ladner was one of the greatest guys I've ever met. He had a good head on his shoulders and whenever he talked, I always wanted to listen. I mean, he was the coolest guy ever. I wish that everybody in the world could have met him. He was always smiling, and if you'd ever met him, he'd put a smile on your face, too."

"I'm not worried as far as securing a job after I finish my career in the military, I know, with all due respect, that the only thing I'll probably have to worry about is how I might react to civilians. They don't understand the whole concept of military bearing. Unless you've been there..."

"Being so young when he joined the Marines, Brandon went through his experiences and got out and before I ever left for mine. He had no problem sharing that. I mean, he went all the way down to the nitty gritty. He told us all the little facts that we needed to know. The most important thing he showed me was that life was not worth going through angry or mad, just smile and get through it. I have to admit; that's how I try to live my life. I've modeled it after Brandon. He taught us all some serious life lessons." Alex Kenner paused and took a deep breath. "I know I'll see him again one day."

☐

-Steve Kenner-

"Nobody will ever replace Brandon. Nobody."

"I first met Brandon Ladner at our home. It was right around the time our son Alex graduated high school. Brandon had come over for the graduation party we'd held. (We liked knowing who Alex's friends were.) Right from the start, my wife and I took notice of Brandon. He was polite, a real "Yes sir" and "No ma'am" type of young man. I guess we hadn't met him until that stage of the game for the fact that that he bounced back and forth between high Pelham and Thompson schools."

When asked to describe Brandon, Mr. Kenner gave the question much thought and consideration before answering. "There was always something about him that stood out. Brandon was a combination of many things. He was excitable and funny, but he was also a proud young man. His personality traits were all positive. Brandon was a tremendous pleasure to be around. The sad part about everything was that he was always the life of the party, the guy that everybody enjoyed being around."

"Brandon had such an amazing persona. He was a good person and loved being around people. He put off a good vibe. You could see the kind of person he was by watching the people he surrounded himself with. He valued his friendships. What I saw from his friends was that he always lived life to its fullest. Brandon always wanted to have fun."

"I don't have too many stories to share. I mean, I enjoyed meeting the people our son was friends with, but you know, I was 'Dad.' Alex would always say, 'Get out of here' when his friends dropped by." Mr. Kenner laughed easily. "I do have one story I can share. Alex had all of them over here for a poker game. They'd been playing awhile and decided to take a break. Of course, they'd been drinking beer, you know, just having a guy's night out together. Mike Linder had a beard at the time, and they'd talked him into shaving it into a Fu Manchu. They took pictures of the entire process and posted them on Facebook. Brandon had been here many times of course, but that poker game was probably one of the funniest times."

"I remember exactly what I was doing the day I found out what happened. Talk about shocked. I'd been here at the house when Drew Dudley posted about it on line. I couldn't believe it. I'd just seen Brandon and had invited him over to the house. We hadn't seen him for a while you know, on account of our son having joined the Air Force. We pretty much lost touch with all the boys."

"I'd heard about that number 'twenty-two a day', about soldiers coming home and taking their own lives. From like 2007 or 2008, the problem increased. I would have never thought Brandon to be one to do that. He kept it hidden well, but some of his friends had noticed it. Alex told me how some of the guys they worked out with had noticed that Brandon had grown quiet at the gym. Brandon had always been laughing and joking around before, but something had changed."

"The times I was around him, Brandon was always full of life. He was so funny, I mean, the kind of person you just wanted to be around. I'm so glad that my son had him in his life, both of them so proud to serve their country. Brandon cared. He was genuinely concerned about others. You don't see a lot of younger people like that. Men can have feelings too. It's such a shame what happened. Brandon was a great example of what bond a friendship could be. His death affected my son Alex. It's not the same when all the guys all get together now, something is missing. There's a void. Nobody will ever replace Brandon Ladner: nobody. He was a very unique individual."

-Elaine Plowman-
"We can't bring him back, but we can remember."

"The first time that I met Brandon was when my son Zachary started at Thompson High School in Alabaster, Alabama. Zachary came home one day and told me, 'Mom, I met a kid today (Brandon), and I'm not sure we're going to get along.' So I tried reassuring him by telling him, 'You're the new kid. Don't worry about who's going to pick on you. It happens to all the new kids.' Time went on and the next thing you know, Brandon was coming over to the house. He was one of the kids who had said something to Zachary but never meant any harm by it. When Brandon came to the house, he was all like, "Welcome to Thompson" and our family just took him in as one of our own."

"Brandon would come over every day after school and even stay for dinner at times. We enjoyed having him. He was one of those kids who had a great heart. He always said 'Thank you,' 'No ma'am,' and 'Yes sir' and always called us by our last names. Brandon was just naturally respectful. He was always welcome at our house. His mom Renee and I were considered second moms to one another's boys. He went by and respected the rules at our house but of course, they were typical teenage boys, and when he stayed over, they occasionally tried sneaking out late at night."

"One time, I received a call at two in the morning. It was Brandon. He'd call me like that if there was something going on or if he knew his mom was going to be out of town. The boys never did anything horrible, nothing to get real excited about but one night, he called from some party that he and a whole bunch of other kids were at. They were partying in this empty house that one of their friends had moved from. It was nothing major but somebody had called the cops on them and Brandon got caught. He didn't want his mom to know about it so there I go, down to the police station to get him. I acted like I was Renee and was all stern with him as I took him home. The next morning, of course, I had to have a conversation with him."

"Kids in the neighborhood were always coming over to our house to hang out. We let them do pretty much what they wanted, and they never did anything we didn't approve of. Everybody knew I was always watching from the sidelines, like a shadow in the dark. As a matter of fact, Brandon once said, 'Every time we turn around, there you are.' I always tried to be there for them no matter what. I wanted them to know I had their backs 24/7, keeping them straight. I think they all respected the fact that I was that kind of mom. Renee's the same way, always keeping the boys in line."

"Adjectives." After giving the matter some thought, Ms. Plowman responded. "Well, lovable is the first one that comes to mind. Brandon was one big, lovable boy. He had a heart of gold, pure gold. He never met a stranger and always wanted to help people. 'I don't mind helping. What do you need me to do?' He was always smiling, always joking and doing his good-natured picking a lot. He loved making people laugh."

"Brandon had traveled to Kentucky for my son's wedding. He was still joking and laughing away just like the Brandon we had grown to love. On this occasion, he'd ridden with me to the ceremony. 'Is it okay if I smoke?' he asked. I didn't care, so he lit one up. 'Do you have something I can put this out in or you want me just to throw it out the window?' I told him to just throw it out. Of course, it came right back in. I was driving and we were trying to look around and find where it landed. We made it back to the house and I got out and looked in the back of the SUV, and there it was. It hadn't burned anything and Brandon was like, 'Thank God you found it.' There were all kinds of things like that."

"Brandon bought a dirt bike so he and Zachary would go out back and ride up and down the yard. We had a big strip out back that had a water plant behind it and they rode out there a lot. I remember one time when Brandon was popping wheelies, he ended up wrecking. It was a few weeks after that incident when Brandon came into the house looking a little upset. He asked me to come outside and sit with him. That's when he started talking about joining the Marines."

"Brandon thought he wanted to get away for a little while and was ready to move on somewhere challenging so he wouldn't get into trouble at home. I supported his decision. He'd said, 'Me, Zach, and Johnny talked about joining at the same time so we'd all be together.' I told him that wasn't how things worked. When Brandon joined, Johnny joined shortly after that and my son went right after that. They were sent all over the place, of course, but I kept in touch with Brandon while he was in Afghanistan. All the times I talked with him, he seemed like he was exactly where he wanted to be."

"Brandon came home from overseas and we set out on the front porch and talked about where he'd been, how he loved his job and how he'd do it all again. I asked him if everything was okay, and of course, he said he was fine but had seemed a little standoffish, so unlike Brandon. I kept watching him because I knew something was wrong but I didn't know what was going on. I wasn't sure if it was girl issues or what, but when he came to visit with us, he seemed distant. I couldn't understand what was going on."

"I realized PTSD might have been there, but thought, 'No, this can't be.' Brandon wasn't the type of person to be down or stressed or depressed. I believed him when he told me he was fine but then a couple of weeks later, he and his girlfriend of the time had broken up and he started dating another girl. I asked him again if he was okay and he assured me he was fine. He promised. It wasn't very long after that when we got the news. That was devastating. I sat back and I thought about all the little signs I saw but didn't know, then felt so bad. I saw it, I saw it in him. That was the sad part. Not only was it sad, but now I worry about my own son because he lost his best friend and was in that same environment. Sometimes I think I see the same things in my son that I saw in Brandon. I feel something could go wrong. Zachary thinks about Brandon a lot, how much he misses him."

"When Brandon came to visit, the boys got out on their dirt bikes just like they'd done back in Alabama. I enjoyed that; those moments with Brandon. It makes me smile to know my son and he were close. Their friendship turned out well. Zachary held onto that bike until just the end of this past November. It was the last bike Brandon rode. I know my son held on to it for as long as he could."

"My first thought when I found out what happened was, 'Why?' I didn't understand. I was so shocked but I wasn't. I was frustrated, wondering why these guys don't have the help that they need. I feel the military should keep these boys a little longer when they come back. It was so sad yet at the same time, it made me angry. I mean, it just wasn't in Brandon. He was too sweet, too full of life. That's the sad part, for things like this to happen; it affects people you wouldn't think it could."

"Brandon's death was devastating. He was extremely well-liked and had so many friends. Everybody enjoyed being around him. Out of all my kids' friends, Brandon was always so polite and mannerly about things. He knew he could walk right in our door without knocking. He just had that way about him. He was a good kid, was good for my kids and I was happy to have him stay here any time he wanted."

"Brandon was tremendously loved. I felt like his death wasn't real, that it didn't really happen. The day we found out, I went straight over to my sons' house, my daughter came over and we all just sat on the porch and cried. Zachary hit rock bottom that day. I listened to him talk about all the good things that he and Brandon had shared together. He couldn't understand why his best friend had taken his own life."

"I remember my daughter had just had her baby and Brandon was so excited to come visit. When he saw the baby, he was all like, *'Which way do you hold her?'* He was so cute. The day Brandon left, he came over to the house. *'Can I get a picture with you and Zachary?'* We were all standing out on the sidewalk and he smiled so big. I think about that and wonder why he felt like he had to ask? I thought it was peculiar. There was so much going on that week when my son married."

"One time, we had a dog named Snoopy who was not nice to anybody, until Brandon came along. As a matter of fact, Brandon's girlfriend Rachel came into the house for something or other one time and Snoopy bit her, but Brandon? He could walk in without any problem. We'd tell him to watch out for Snoopy because it would bite but he came in and stooped down, Snoopy sniffed at him and they were good to go. Brandon was like, 'I don't have to worry. I can just walk on in the house. This dog isn't going to bite me.' Snoopy loved Brandon. We could never let the dog out because he always wanted to bite. Kids in the neighborhood would be like, 'Snoopy's mean. He bites' but not Brandon. The boys would always come running to the house whenever they wanted to get away from a girl or a crowd because they knew Snoopy would keep everybody away."

"Twenty-two; that number makes me sick on the inside, it makes me physically ill. These young men sacrificed a part of their lives for this country and they can't get that back. Brandon's death affected so many people in so many ways. Today, I worry about my own son. I know he's still hurting over Brandon's loss. Hopefully, things will work out in the long run, but losing Brandon was a very big deal for us all. I know we can't bring him back but we can remember."

☐

-Amber Gowens-

"He was that person you could tell anything to and he'd help you through it."

"I'd moved from Hawaii in 2000 and lived in Alabama for about a year. Brandon and I met in 2002 after my brother had brought him to the house. Those two were best friends. At the time, we were all still in school. I was in middle school and they were in high school."

"Brandon was a 'steady' in our life. Being a military family ourselves, it was difficult to connect with people on the level most kids get to bond on because of us having to move every three years, but Brandon was someone who automatically fit in with our family, just like he'd been with us our whole lives. Even after we moved from Alabama, we kept in contact through Facebook, phone calls, and texting."

"My brother and Brandon were never far from each other. If you saw Zac, you knew Brandon wasn't far behind and vice versa. Our house was the hang-out spot after school before the boys went to work. We always had a good time, laughing, arguing about things we agreed or disagreed on or just hanging out wasting time (moments that I will always hold close to me)."

"When Brandon came to Kentucky for my older brother's wedding, it had been the first time in about six years that we had seen him. (He and my brother had been deployed in the Marines.) It was an extra special occasion for my family to have Brandon there with us. I tried to spend as much time with him as I could, staying up way past bedtime, talking about life and how he'd been doing. We reminisced about the lively boy we'd all known in our teen years to how we'd watched him grow up and talking about real life. We talked about the problems and choices and about how he didn't feel like he was anywhere on the map. Brandon was indeed still that lively boy, just older, a lot louder, but also very serious."

"The last conservation he and I had took place on my mom's front porch. Brandon told me how proud he was of the person that I had become, commented on how beautiful my children were and how he planned to visit more often. He loved our whole family. Brandon wasn't just a friend or someone I've known for a long time. He was more like a big brother. He was family in every sense of the word. I will never forget all the truly good times we had, all the good 'heart to hearts' or kicks in the butt he gave when I needed them. This man meant more to me than anybody knows."

"Brandon was so full of life. He was that person that you could tell anything to and he'd help you through it. He was honest and truthful but most of all, he was very funny." Amber grew silent as she gave much thought to the next question. When asked about an outstanding quality about Brandon, she immediately responded, "His sense of humor and his goofiness. In any situation, he could make you laugh."

"I remember one time when I was getting ready to fight with somebody for some reason or another and Brandon was all like, 'Amber. You don't have to do this. I'll take you home.' He was like my big brother, always there for me. There was another time when I'd been sitting on the hood of a truck and fell off. I got hurt pretty bad and he was the only one who took it seriously. I ended up breaking a small bone in my ankle and couldn't walk so he carried me back home. The whole time, he kept asking if I was okay or if I was hurting. Brandon was kind and concerned. He was a great guy."

"When I first found out that he was gone, my first thought was, 'of all people, why him?' For somebody like Brandon to do something like that was so shocking. He was so full of life and always so happy. He made other people happy."

"I'm from a military family so I sort of knew about the twenty-two a day but I didn't know the exact number/statistic. I still haven't found any sense of closure to all of this."

☐

-Terry Dyess-

"If Brandon gave you his word, you'd know come hell or high water, he'd get it done."

Asked when he first met Brandon, Terry Dyess responded, "I have to think about this a minute. I grew up with Brandon's mother, Renee. She lived just around the corner from us back in the day. I didn't meet Brandon until somewhere around the spring of 2011 or 2012." Mr. Dyess paused. "It was right about the time I was going through a divorce. I was in a bad situation. Well, Renee and I had kept touch via Facebook. They were living in Alabama at the time. I was having a particularly rough day when she offered, 'Come on over and see us.' When I got there, that's when I met Brandon. Long story short, I ended up living in Alabama and got to know Brandon pretty well."

"Brandon was a good person, such a joy to be around." Terry exhaled slowly. "I'd describe him as being a loyal guy who had a lot of integrity. He was friendly, of course. I mean, Brandon never met a stranger. He had a way of putting people at ease from the start. As I'm thinking of this, let me tell you. There were many years difference in our ages, but we'd sit around talking as if we were the best of friends. He was that way with everybody. That reminds me: there was this one time where he and I were sitting around, having drinks and just shooting the bull. As we were sitting there, I looked at him and straight up told him that I hoped my own son grew up to be half the man that he was. Brandon sat there a second and kind of took all that in. He stood up, leaned over and shook my hand and said, 'I really appreciate that.' Most guys would've just blown that comment off: not Brandon."

"When Brandon said something, you could take it to the bank. If he gave you his word, you could know that come hell or high water, he'd get it done. And bonfires, he loved bonfires. He'd dug this huge pit behind one of his friend's houses. We'd all sit out there for hours, drinking beer, talking. He'd get on Facebook and invite everybody he knew to come to one of his bonfires. He nicknamed me 'The Mayor.' I think we'd had a little too much to drink and that just came up from off the top of his head. I mean, that was just Brandon."

"When I first heard about what had taken place, I was in Houston. I saw something on Facebook, so I texted Renee. My first reaction was disbelief. Oh my God, why? I never saw it coming. There'd been a few times I thought that Brandon had something bothering him but he always kept it contained. I almost feel like he must have thought it'd be a sign of weakness if he discussed it. He didn't want to be 'that' guy. That was something he perceived as making him a failure. Brandon loved, loved the Corps. He was a Marine's Marine. The kid was so smart. He was schooling for nursing, and he was doing well with that, changing majors along the line somewhere."

"Twenty-two a day: I didn't know anything about it before Brandon. I think it's a damn disgrace though that our government doesn't seem to want to do anything for our Veterans: what they have to go through even to be seen. I know they say there's help out there, resources but if they (the VA) claim they are backlogged. My question is if they were so damn backlogged, they should have allowed those guys to seek private care. Twenty-two a day turns my stomach."

"I think of that kid every day. When I found out about Brandon, I mean, there was no outward sign. I guess he had it all compartmentalized. I would never have guessed. He was so outgoing and friendly, seemed to have everything together. I guess all the little things built up."

"The world became a sadder place when he left it. It felt a little darker the day I found out." Mr. Dyess stopped abruptly as he caught his breath. "There was honest to God nothing negative about the man. This whole situation made me take pause and take notice of what our military has done and continues to do to the guys who fight for this country. They're kids, not grown men when they go to war. For the government to chew them up and spit them out makes me ill. Here you go, off to war with you and when you come home, here's your discharge paper, b-bye."

☐

-Adam Ellis-

"Brandon was a pretty dependable person all the way around."

"I first met Brandon back when were both in the 9th grade. He'd moved from Pelham over to Thompson, and we met through a mutual friend of ours, Zac Scott. Brandon used to hang with Zac after school all the time and so that's how we met."

Giving much consideration before answering the next question, Mr. Ellis was asked how he'd describe Brandon to a stranger. "I'd describe Brandon as out-going, almost hyper. He loved to laugh, and he joked around all the time. A couple of particularly outstanding qualities I would use to describe him would be his loyalty and honesty. Brandon was both, a pretty dependable person all the way around."

"There are so many stories I could share." Mr. Ellis paused as he thought about what to say next. "One time, Brandon and his family invited me to go with them to the beach. We were out there having a good time but had to pack up early because some hurricane came in, I can't remember which one it was, but there we all were, in Panama City headed up to Atlanta to go to Six Flags while that hurricane was ready to come through. We were just concerned with getting to Six Flags and weren't too worried about the wind."

"I was having issues with some old friends. So, I got on Facebook to talk with some people and you know, Brandon was the only person from my past to reach out. He knew I was having troubles and invited me over to talk. I'd been away for a long time. Coming home was just coming back to a place and to people that had changed so much. That was the last time I had a chance to speak with him before he passed away."

"Brandon never came right out and said anything, but I felt like something had happened, that something had changed him. We used to hang out a lot, but I guess time changed us all." Mr. Ellis paused with his thoughts before continuing quietly. "When I found out what happened to Brandon, I was in shock. I mean, I couldn't believe it. I found out through my mother. She'd stopped by the post office and found out, you know, Brandon used to work there. Like I said, he and I had visited not too long before everything happened. I never thought Brandon was the kind of guy to go out like that, that this was what would have happened, of all things." Mr. Ellis paused again. "I mean sure, Brandon was intense at times, but he was a genuinely a good person."

-Cassie Lasabbe-

"Brandon was a very comfortable person to be around."

"Brandon was my brother. Any time I had a break-up in high school or something, he'd be all like, '*What's going on?*' If I had to describe him to a stranger, well, I wouldn't want to scare anybody, but I'd tell them Brandon was a good-crazy, always playing jokes on people, always making inside jokes, outgoing, respectful," Cassie paused. "-he'd never make you feel awkward though, even if you had just met him. Brandon was a comfortable person to be around."

Giving much thought to answering the next question, Ms. Lasabbe was asked about Brandon's most outstanding quality. "He was honest, but maybe more amazing was how he had this great ability to put people at ease. All in all, he was tactful and very heartfelt. He never put out that 'I'm a tough-guy' persona. Brandon was very personable."

"Let me tell you a story of just an ordinary thing. Me, my cousin Laney, Ashley, Brandon, and Jamy we all went to the Cahaba River. Everybody wanted to float. That's just something they do in Alabama. Well, I'd never done such a thing. So there we all were, going to float the river. Brandon had us take this rinky-dink truck up to the beginning of the river. We got down to the water and started pulling our ice-chests and beer down to the water's edge and I noticed the water was green. I didn't want anything to do with that and asked Brandon what we were floating in. Long story short, Ashley and Brandon talked us all into floating. We were settling into floating down this lovely green river when from out of nowhere, a snake came flying across the water. So there we were, trying to flip out of the tubes with good ole Brandon trying to control the chaos and keep us from jumping out. I told him I was never going with him down the river again. That's still one of my favorite times, though."

"I remember another time when Brandon had this beautiful car, an Acura I think. He and I went to the grocery store for one thing or another. I didn't have a driver's license at the time but after we'd got down there and picked up whatever it was we'd gone shopping for, Brandon let me drive. Of course, he made me stop before we got home so we could switch drivers but I thought that was cool for him to do that."

"When Brandon died, I was still in college at the time. My aunt called and she was crying hysterically. She told me I had to come home immediately and of course, my first thought was that something had happened to my child. 'No. It's Brandon'. She told me what happened and I couldn't believe it. I called my best friend and talked with her all the way home. It didn't make any sense to me. Brandon was never that kind of person. Why? Why somebody so full of life would ever do that? There had to have been so many things on his mind that he just didn't share with people. He wanted to protect others from the things he had experienced I guess. We didn't know there was ever anything wrong."

"Before all this, I knew nothing about twenty-two people a day. Many people still don't know this is happening. It's crazy. Brandon was that guy who was always trying to fix the troubles that everybody else was having. I could always talk to him about anything. He'd always assure me that everything was going to be okay."

-Lorianne Wood-

"There was no warning, and that's scary."

"I was the aunt who was closest to Renee's kids when they were little. While we were all growing up, I'd always wanted to be around my big sister Renee, so I was always babysitting the kids. Brandon was her youngest: my beautiful nephew. He wasn't Brandon to me, though. He was Boo-Boo. Even when I speak of him now, it's still about Boo-Boo. I was Aunt Lo-Lo. Everybody knew Brandon as this big, strong Marine, but to me, he was always Boo-Boo."

"I could share so many stories about Brandon." There was a long pause before Lorianne continued. "I get upset talking about him. I don't know where to pull any of those stories from without getting sad." Lorianne paused again. "Renee might have given him the name 'Brandon,' but for the first five or six weeks of his life, we all called him 'Sgt. Carter.' When Boo-Boo was born, he had this head full of black hair. We called him Sgt. Carter because he looked just like that sergeant on Gomer Pyle, that old television series with Jim Nabors. This was long before Boo ever thought about joining the military himself. Of course, his pet names changed quite a bit as he grew up." Lorianne laughed in fond reverie. "We called him Boo-Boo, then as he got older, his name changed to Rooty: 'Rooty-Tooty, Fresh and Fruity.'"

"It's easy to describe Brandon. He was outgoing, funny, outrageous, loving, and family-oriented. I can't even tell you his most outstanding quality. It's still hard. There are too many things, too many outstanding qualities to name just one. He was a lover of life, of people, that's for sure."

179

"Brandon's first dirty martini was courtesy of Aunt Lo. I lived with my mom to help take of her and she and I were always drinking them with Brandon. It turned out to be his favorite drink."

"Have you ever seen his baby pictures? Brandon was such a big baby that he seemed to have no neck when he was born. That was part of why we called him Sgt. Carter for a brief time. Even when he was a baby, Brandon's disposition was infectious, completely intoxicating. He was the cutest and sweetest thing you ever did see."

"Renee and I were close. I always looked up to her. She was such a good mother. Brandon was her favorite. We connected with Brandon. I was always so worried about him when he was racing his bikes, always so scared he'd wreck or hurt himself but he always came out on top, no matter what he tried to do. Then he went into the Marines. How do you go from that to that? There were so many times I just prayed. I mean, I didn't know if he was going to die then, and he didn't. You know, now there are lots of people who ask about how he died. The war caught him. It was later, but it got him, long after he came home."

"When I found out what had happened, my first thoughts were for Renee. I couldn't understand her when she called to tell us but I knew what happened just from the emotion in her call. I couldn't tell you the exact words she said, but I know I wanted to go to her immediately. I had to do what I had to do and me and our mom went to her (and mom didn't usually leave the house for anything). I can't know how Renee felt. I always wanted to be around her because of Brandon. Myself, I have five, beautiful, healthy children and couldn't imagine losing one of them. I don't know what I'd do if I ever lost a child. Hearing my sister's emotions at the end of that phone call was life-changing for me."

"I think twenty-two a day is unacceptable. It's neglectful, I don't know what anyone is doing about it, I don't know how we could have prevented Brandon's death, but we should have. There was no warning though, and that's the scary part. There might have been, but we never saw it. We never expected it to happen to Brandon. He was the funniest guy on the planet."

Continuing her highly emotional interview, Lorianne described her nephew. "Boo-Boo was always a 'glass half-full' kind of guy. He always saw the positive side of everything. We always had so much fun. I remember one occasion that we'd spent time together back when I lived in West Virginia. Brandon came up and saw his first waterfall. We'd hiked down to the back of those falls and stood behind them. We were both like, 'Thank you God.' I mean, to be standing there and sharing that moment together with Brandon? It was so beautiful. It was such a good Thanksgiving."

"I remember Brandon said this one time: 'I want everybody to know, I wish I could change the world, if I could join the military and be a Marine, I might change the world for about a minute.' I remember him and his Motocross, and then suddenly he wanted to be a Marine. I asked him, 'why do you want to be a Marine?' and he said, 'I want to defend my country, and I want to change the world.'"

-Kathy Angel Plemons-

"I'll always remember Brandon as the cute little boy with a great big smile and sparkly blue eyes who was always happy to be wherever he was."

"It was 1996, and we'd just moved to the Pelham, Alabama area. My son Tyler met Brandon when they started third grade at Valley Elementary. The boys were in school together and I was one of those parents who were always helping out, many times as a room mom. A couple of years later, they both had Mrs. Emily Blount for one of their fifth-grade teachers. Most of the memories I have of the boys were from that time because there was such a tremendous combination of activities going on. I mean, they participated in everything that year. They completed an in-depth study of Colonial Williamsburg, attended the Governors Ball and took one unforgettable class trip to Washington, D. C. all in the same year. I went on that trip as well and had the pleasure of chaperoning the group Brandon and Tyler were in."

"Brandon Ladner always loved to make others laugh. He was a mischievous and playful person. At that time, Brandon was small in stature but that never stopped him from leading the way. His precocious manner was never lost on anyone. All the little girls thought that he was so cute and he sure enough was. (Brandon always took care to make sure his hair was styled with precision.) Kim Ellison, a mother of one of Brandon's classmates, made the remark about how Brandon's energy was so contagious to everyone on that trip. "His energy kept us all going strong.""

One of Kathy Plemon's clearest memories of Brandon was from the time their family took him with them to the circus.

"One year, near the end of January, we took the boys to the circus at the BJCC (Birmingham Jefferson Civic Center) Arena in downtown Birmingham. They had a great time. That trip was fun for all of us, and even though the boys were fifth-graders, they still loved playing with the swords and little lights that we'd purchased for them at the event. It was all such fun."

"Our house seemed to be the 'go-to' place in the neighborhood. We had the big yard and a pool so of course we'd have the pool parties, the birthday parties, and sports parties which were all celebrated quite often. In the fall, everybody looked forward to our camping parties. We had open campfires where we'd toast marshmallows and have plenty of fireworks. Of course, no party was complete without an obligatory drive-by from the local police who made sure all was well. Our wonderful neighbors were always watching out for us."

Garrett Knox, childhood friend of Brandon's, relayed this to Kathy: "Brandon had a good heart. One of the positive things I remember best about him was how anytime anybody got hurt playing ball, Brandon would be the first one making sure the injured party was 'good to go.' He could be tough, but he'd be the first guy to make sure everyone was okay."

Teacher Emily Blount remembers Brandon as being playful, energetic and always in the middle of everything. "On the trip to Washington, D.C. the boys were so excited about everything and they had so much fun." She stated. "The boys were so enthusiastic each day as new adventures awaited them." Upon learning of Brandon's passing, she remarked, "It was a heartfelt loss to our small community. I felt so much sympathy for his family."

Marva Garland, mother of Brandon's childhood friend Glenn Sadler, stated how proud she was of Brandon's service to our country and remarked that he had truly given his all. "Glenn, Tyler, Garrett, Matt and all the boys were friends with Brandon. They were all so sad to hear the news. His passing hit home hard. There were no words."

Kathy recalled when she'd first heard the news of Brandon's death. She talked about how she had discussed his passing with her own son Tyler. "My heart broke. Tyler and I couldn't believe it. We were just so sad for his mom and family. I remember saying to Tyler, 'I don't know how a mother is supposed to live through something like this.' Tyler had told family friend Kim Ellison, 'If he had just waited five minutes or had gone to sleep...'"

"In answering the question about the statistic twenty-two a day; "I never knew what that number meant, and unfortunately, now we all do. It's still so unbelievable but yet so real. The price a country pays for war is obviously a never-ending one. Does anyone really know what a family, this family, his mother, his brother, his sister still have to go through in their lifetimes because of PTSD and what it has done to them? The real question (and real sadness) is 'what did Brandon and so many others like him go through before they got to that point? That's what has to be 'fixed' before it is too late."

"I'll always remember Brandon Ladner as the cute little boy with the great big smile and sparkling blue eyes who was so always happy to be wherever he was. Thanks, Brandon. I'm glad we broke the rules and used the phone to call home!"

-Jonathan Haltiwanger-

"That was who he was: always bringing people together."

"Brandon and I first met back in the old neighborhood in Pelham, Alabama. I think he was maybe eight or nine years old at the time."

Jonathan didn't take any pause before answering the question of how he'd describe Brandon. "Goodhearted, definitely goodhearted. He cared deeply about friends and family, and you know, he absolutely loved the Marine Corps. That's probably the best way I can describe him. Brandon had a lot of heart. I mean, he was an upbeat and caring kind of guy and when it came right down to it, he was *always* a good friend. He was very intelligent too, but-" Jonathan paused "-he had a good head on his shoulders." Jonathan chuckled before finishing his description "He was some ladies' man, too. Ever since I first met him, he *always* had a girlfriend."

"Do I have a story to share? Yes, yes I do. I'll tell you about the time we were in Panama City, Florida. I remember we were driving down some strip on the beach, more like crawling along about two miles an hour. There was so much traffic, never mind the number of people all over the place. My cousin was driving and I remember people just walking right in front of the car like no big deal. Well, it *was* a big deal. For whatever reason, my cousin had let off the breaks and ended up tapping this one guy who I guess didn't notice a car was trying to drive through. It was on then. It seemed like all of the sudden, these other guys were jumping out from the sidelines along the road and started trying to pull the car doors open, wanting to start throwing punches. Before I knew it, along came Brandon and what does he do? In one punch, he knocked out the guy who'd started it all: one punch."

"There were security guards all over the place. Long story short, there goes Brandon. The security guard who'd gotten hold of him told him "come with me" while he called the police. Brandon respected authority so much that he went right along with the guy just like he was told. I mean, the guard was calling the cops to arrest him. Well, there I was telling Brandon that the guy was only a security guard and we needed to get out of there. "We need to leave: right now!" Brandon stood up and the guard was just beside himself, telling us, "You need to come back." I was like, 'No we don't' but there'd been ole Brandon, just sitting there waiting for the cops to show, doing what he was told. He was going to sit right there and wait."

"When all that happened in Panama, I think Brandon was only seventeen. The guy he knocked out was around twenty-five. You have to understand something. Even at that age, Brandon was built like a tug boat. He was strong. I mean, he probably could've been a great football player but he liked the military."

"When I found out what had happened to Brandon, my first thought was that my boy Morris was kidding with me or he had been misinformed; that's what I was hoping anyway. It wasn't long before I realized the news was true. I'd been working (at a job Brandon had gotten me) so I immediately told the lady in HR. She'd known Brandon, too and told me to take all the time off I needed."

"I'd had a cousin (who was in the Army) who had taken his life in Afghanistan so I knew a little about the whole twenty-two a day thing but not a whole lot. I knew it was a problem. Brandon had talked to me about things before, about when he was in Iraq. I wasn't a fellow Veteran but he talked about a lot of stuff. He told me about the sleep issues he'd started having after he came back-" Jonathan paused. "If I could see him again, I'd tell him how much we all loved him."

"The last time he came home from over across, I remember going to the house for his welcome home party. Everybody was there, and we were all having a good time. I mean, everybody loved Brandon. That homecoming brought everybody together. I remember sitting there that night thinking how the Marines had turned him into a man." Jonathan paused again after an unanticipated moment of silence. When he spoke again, his voice had softened, wrought with sincere emotion. "Even at his funeral, there were so many people; more people there than I had ever seen at any other service. Everybody had such heavy hearts because Brandon was no longer with us. He'd have been proud to see us all together. That was who he was, always bringing people together."

☐

-Rachel Argo-

"Men were willing to give their lives for this country yet the VA won't give those men thirty minutes."

"I first met Brandon in the halls of Thompson High School. We were between classes, and it was only him and I out there. He'd just moved to the area and it was his first day. He'd hollered at me from down the hall. I guess from a distance, he thought I was somebody he knew from Pelham. He had this sneaky grin and ended up giving me a simple hello after he saw I wasn't who he'd thought I was. That was all I saw of him until school let out. I'd gone home and was walking out of the house for something or other and saw Brandon across the street at a friend's house. At first, I thought he was following me but he'd actually befriended my neighbor earlier that day at school."

"Brandon was witty. I mean, he was hilarious. He was also honest. Brandon would look people in the eye and say exactly what he had to say. He was very vocal but was also caring and understanding. He was an outgoing, people-person and was never judgmental. I'd have to say he could talk to anybody and make them feel better regardless of their situation. He'd always make things seem like they were going to be okay even if they weren't. The way Brandon was, after he'd talk with you about whatever you needed to talk about, you'd have peace for a little while."

"I remember one time we'd had a party at my house. There were maybe a hundred people there. My dad ended up busting the party. I didn't know it at the time but Brandon hadn't left when everybody else scattered. He'd hidden when my dad came in and didn't leave until about two hours later. He didn't want my dad to know that he'd been part of the party."

"After Brandon died, Renee told me what happened. At first, I thought it was a joke. My first thoughts were to think that maybe if we hadn't gotten into a fight before I left, it might not have happened. Brandon had commented to me that he sometimes felt suicidal, especially after some of our fights but everything always turned out fine and he'd be back to his old self. He'd assure me I was his soul mate and that we were going to get married, have kids and live the whole happily ever after."

"Twenty-two a day; that number makes me angry. I feel the VA has failed our Veterans. They haven't given them the proper tools to adapt to civilian life. Those who train, go overseas and do and witness the things that our Vets do, I feel it takes a toll. These people have to be rewired and when everything is said and done, the military sends them home, sends them on their way and tells them if they have any problems, go to their local VA."

"Let me tell you something. I took Brandon to the VA. They never spent more than ten minutes with him before sending him on his way. They'd mail him whatever prescriptions they thought he needed to take and, everything seemed so unorganized. It was ridiculous. I think the longest time he ever spent talking to anybody up there might have been 20 minutes. The doctors and psychiatrists there, you think they'd be able to talk to them whenever these guys needed to, but Brandon sure didn't have that. He was basically told, "Deal with it." These Vets were willing to give their lives for this country yet the VA won't give them 20 minutes?"

"Brandon never wanted to be the focus of any attention or for people to worry about him. On some levels, you'd see it in him that something had changed but he'd put up a front, smile and laugh it off. Most of the time he'd keep things bottled up but he'd still have those moments behind closed doors. Brandon was very private. There were few people he would talk to. I think he came home a completely different person and just didn't want anybody to know what was going on in his mind. I think he felt this stigma that despite what he had done overseas as a strong and capable Marine that he should have been able to deal with things back home just fine. We need to change that."

-Joel Doss-

"...a very bright light in a very dark world burned out."

"I could never forget meeting a guy like Brandon. He was the type who let everybody know how cool he thought they were. Back in high school, I remember this young kid yelling my name from across the lunchroom. It was Brandon, and for some reason, I guess he thought I was some kind of cool guy. I don't know why, but he thought I was. (I happened to have been dating some of the girls he'd thought were good-looking, so maybe that was it.)" Joel laughed at the memory. "I just remember him yelling my name. 'Why does this kid think I'm so cool?' Next thing I know, we were exchanging phone numbers. The Internet was just kicking off at that time and cell phones didn't exist like they do now. It was a time when people actually socialized with each other. I can't remember who called who first, but our friendship took off."

"I found out he had a dirt bike: a Yamaha. Brandon was always coming over to the house on that bike, pretty late sometimes, too just to hang out. We had a powerline/gas line going on out in our woods, so it was a favorite spot of his to ride. I was working a job while we were in school, so sometimes when I came home, he'd be out there just sitting in the driveway waiting. He took me for a ride on that bike one time and scared the living shit out of me in the process. This guy had no fear: completely 110% fearless. Fear wasn't a word in Brandon's vocabulary. This guy would quite literally do anything he was told to do. I imagine that was what attracted him to the Marine Corps. He was going to do what Brandon wanted to do, whatever Brandon thought was fun. He just did what he was going to do. That's what I remember most."

"Aside from his fearlessness, he was a compassionate person. Brandon never met a stranger, and he didn't judge anybody by any measure. He liked everybody, didn't have any enemies. Brandon was about people; he loved people."

"Another thing I remember (and I don't think his mom even knows about this)..." Joel paused. "He and I grew up in Alabaster Alabama. Honestly, one of THE biggest house parties in our neighborhood happened because of him. Things were happening in my family and essentially we had to sell the house I had grown up in and move. So I decided to throw a huge house party. I knew the perfect person to tell to invite people, too."

"Brandon was the first person I'd told about this party. The house was empty. 'Invite whoever you want.' I'd told him. The next thing I knew, about 150+ people showed up. I was impressed, most certainly. The driveway was filled with vehicles. There were cars side by side down the road the length of an entire football field: rows and rows of them. We basically had the road entirely blocked off. I'll never forget that. I mean, I was expecting maybe 25-30 people at the most. We were within city limits, so we never did have a bonfire but if he'd had the opportunity, I'm sure Brandon would have lit one up."

"When I initially found out the news about Brandon, I was shocked: that natural, initial human response. I mean, I couldn't believe it. Brandon and I finally had gotten back in touch with each other just before I learned about his death on Facebook. I'd known how he had enlisted in the Corps and we'd lost touch after he deployed to Afghanistan. We'd 'friended' on Facebook and were talking about hanging out and about his journey in life, through combat. We were talking about getting together to hang out and get some beers, you know, just do what buddies do: talk about all that stuff. Next thing I know he starts ignoring my messages and I'm getting zero replies. It was as if he was distancing himself from people. I didn't know what was going on, didn't know what to think. The next thing I saw were pictures of him in his dress uniform and RIP written across the top."

"I got goosebumps, and everything turned slow-motion. I lost a heartbeat and my breath. 'WTF? Is this for real? Am I really reading this?' I just didn't understand how somebody with such a great personality, somebody who'd accomplished so much and had made it home from combat is fine for years would want to end it so sudden like. I can't even begin to describe all the feelings of shock, questioning 'why this?' and 'why that?' I was feeling guilty too: like I hadn't tried hard enough to talk to him. I understood how PTSD worked but not how it felt. If I would have had a better understanding, I feel like I should have tried harder to reach him."

"Brandon was one of the coolest people I have ever met. We hung out together all the time. I like to think I was one of his best friends. I feel like I could have done more, been a better friend. At the time, I didn't know what PTSD could do to a person. The whole event reflects my feelings of guilt."

"Around the time Brandon enlisted in the Marines, I'd intended on enlisting, too. I went to all the workout classes, went to the recruiting office and learned Marine Corps processes. I took the ASVAB and was all ready to enlist but ended up getting denied because of hearing loss. I lost my opportunity to join. I feel like maybe if I'd been able to join, maybe that would have pulled me and Brandon closer, maybe would have made me a little more pro-active, more of a genuine friend. Maybe we could have deployed together, I don't know. I could possibly have been over there with him. That's just one of the many things that cross my mind."

"Twenty-two a day is an alarming number. These guys, our Veterans deserve more than coming back to this country and feeling like nobody cares. It takes and outstanding human being to choose to enlist: especially in the Marines. I mean, anybody who chooses to serve essentially gives up everything about themselves: their personal life, their families, some of their freedoms. It's a sacrifice to sign those papers. It's hard for me to wrap my head around the fact that these men accomplished and achieved so much, survived combat, and then had to fight a much harder battle after they came home. Shooting at people is probably a lot easier than coming back home and feeling like nobody cares. It seems like they lost that sense of comradery and structure after they returned." After a brief pause, Doss continued. "I think it takes a special person to be a Marine."

"When Brandon told me about a few of his Corps experiences, I shared with him how I was heavily pursuing my career in law enforcement. I told him my plans to come back to Birmingham to meet up with him so we could grab a beer together. I told him, 'You used to think I was so cool back in school, but you're the one who's cool. YOU inspired ME to do what I needed to do. We're going to have to celebrate when I graduate from the academy.' The day I graduate, I plan to visit his grave. I'll be in my uniform and have a picture with Brandon. I want to show him, 'Hey I did it.' That would mean a lot to him."

"As I shared before, Brandon and I lost touch with one another after he enlisted. I don't know a lot of the people he most recently associated with. To me, Brandon was just a great person: a great man. I think it would be selfish of people who knew him to not want to talk about him. It's just the right thing to do. It's a touchy topic but it's the right thing to do. Brandon deserves it. They all do. Anybody who has done anything in their lives to better themselves or other people or the world deserves to have words spoken about them. They deserve to be recognized. If people don't want to share their stories, I feel that would be so wrong."

"It's human nature to feel down on yourself sometimes, but also to feel motivated or push yourself into doing things. That's one of the main things about Brandon; he always made me feel like I was somebody that I mattered. I'm sure he was like that with everybody. He always found something he liked in somebody. Brandon knew how to make people feel good about themselves. That's what makes his death so tragic. A bright light in a dark world is gone. I hope this book can reignite that light in some way. Sharing his life, his story will bring a part of that light back. That's what this world needs because it's a very dark place."

"One thing that I've learned about PTSD is that a lot of people claim that these suicides are selfish, insinuating that those who take their own life don't care who they are hurting or leaving behind. One thing that people need to understand is that these guys kill themselves because they believe that not even their friends and family would miss them or care that they're gone. That's how serious mental issues are. I believe if more people become aware, the more likely the number twenty-two would drop."

☐

-Brandon Moore, USMC-

"Friends like Ladner don't come around often. Brandon was a real class-act."

"Brandon Ladner was my first friend when we moved down to Alabaster from up near Birmingham. I knew him through his brother Chris. Brandon became one of my best friends. It was definitely love," Moore laughed as he raised his beer. "-nothing but love."

It was June 11th, the same night following the event held at Alabama's National Cemetery in Montevallo, Alabama. Although prior obligations prevented him from coming to the Honor and Remember flag presentation held earlier that evening, Brandon Moore was able to make the gathering of friends and family that was held at Mr. Bob Lipsey's home.

"Adjectives I would use in describing Brandon," Moore paused. "-hardworking, honest, motivated, loving, compassionate, unselfish, the best all-round person you could ever ask for, and Ladner? He was the smartest man I have ever met." When asked which word best described his friend, Moore answered without any hesitation. "The most notable adjective? I think 'unselfish.'." Moore took a drink from his beer and eased back to share a story.

"I was trapped downtown around four in the morning and needed a ride. Brandon had to go to work the next morning around six but I called him anyway. I was all like, 'Hey Bud. I don't ask you for much, but I need you.' He came right down. He was mad as fire but he was all 'I'd rather pick you up then you get a DUI.' He came and got me, took me to the house, cooked us breakfast then we went to sleep." Moore laughed heartily as he shared the story. His face brightened as a thought crossed his mind. "There's another quality about Brandon. He could cook." Laughing as he nodded his head, Moore echoed his thought. "Brandon sure could cook. Biscuits and gravy was his thing. He made the best biscuits and gravy in Alabama."

"I was at work the day we found out what happened. I was about six months into my new job. I'd noticed that I had four or five missed phone calls from another good buddy of mine. I told everybody at work, 'Hey, I've got to go.' They let me go pick up lunch so I could catch my calls. I'll never forget." Moore paused before continuing. "My buddy called me back thinking I had already heard the news. He asked, 'Did you hear?'"

"Hear what?"

"Brandon. He's gone."

"Brandon who? What are you talking about?"

"Ladner. He's gone."

Moore sat back in silence. "I pulled over and burst out crying. I drove back to the clinic and broke the news to Morgan, another friend I work with. I brought her out, tears in my eyes, and told her 'Listen, Ladner's gone,' and we both broke down crying. Brandon was my best friend in this world. He was the reason I joined the Marine Corps."

"Another buddy of mine (one who'd joined the Army) had gotten out of the military and ended up having problems." Moore took a drink from his beer and continued matter-of-factly. "He ended up killing himself, so as far as the news about Brandon? I'd already been through it, sort of. With Brandon though, everything was so unexpected. When I heard the whole thing about Brandon, I was devastated. He was the happiest, most goal-oriented OCD person I'd ever met in my life. I mean, the man had goals. He was the one who taught me to get my own priorities in order." Moore paused as he switched gears. "It was because of Brandon that I joined the Marines myself. I didn't serve with his unit though. I was with Lima 323, a reserve unit out of Montgomery."

"There's so much I could tell about Brandon. He was a great guy all of the time, but you know, some things I just can't share," Moore laughed heartily. "-I mean things I will take to my grave." Pausing briefly, Brandon Moore's voice took on a more serious tone when he spoke again. "Friends like Ladner don't come around often. Brandon sure was a class-act. I miss him to this day."

"I've dealt with my own demons; particularly while having to deal with all my friends' deaths. I dealt with things in all the wrong ways, but with Brandon, I stayed sober. It's been hard. Brandon would want to see everybody together, celebrating, and being happy. He was never about sad. He was my role model, the reason why I turned my own life around." Moore's eyes watered with tears he refused to let fall. "Brandon and I had a lot of good times. I miss that son-of-a-bitch. Brandon Ladner was easily one of the best human beings I have ever met in my entire life. The guy was awesome, and words could never do justice to the man he was."

☐

-Morris Hodges-

"He got it in his head that he wanted to be a Marine and he was going to do whatever it took to become one."

"When did I first meet Brandon? Hell, I can't put a finger on it. I've known him for fifteen years or longer. I was a little older than he was and went to school with his older brother and sister. Brandon though, he was a tough kid but always smiling. He minded his own business and was just an all-round good guy, the type of friend you didn't have to ask to leave. You know the type. Everybody has one or two of those friends who after a while just get on your nerves? Not Brandon. He was one hell of a friend, the kind you never wanted to leave; he never got on my nerves."

"If things were already going good in your life, Brandon was 'extra.' He'd tell you, 'That is *so* good! Good for you.' If things weren't going so well for you, he cared enough to stop whatever he was doing and see if he could change things around. He was always interested in what was happening to you. And I suppose you know already, Brandon loved dirt bikes. He was the short and stocky dude who could ride like a fool! He'd go driving 80mph down the middle of some back, county road and wouldn't think anything of it."

"I only lived about ten miles down the road from him. So one day, I'd decided I was going to turn my garage into a man cave. Brandon thought that was the greatest idea. I remember it was hotter than hell outside and everybody came down to the 'cave.' Brandon didn't care about how hot it was. He was sitting there happy as hell. I mean, any game that came on, Brandon was over here drinking a beer. It wasn't anything to be outside with him with a set of golf clubs at 2 am hitting balls into the neighbor's yard."

"About a week before he died, we were out in the man cave. It'd been raining so everybody was in there watching Alabama football. Around one o'clock that morning, Brandon came up to me

197

from out of the blue and said, '*I'm proud of you. You've got it going on, man.*' I couldn't figure why he'd say that to me so I answered back, 'No, you're the one who's got it going on.' Looking back, it's something I'll never forget. When he told me that, I was like 'Ok, thanks' but then everything happened and it turned into something pretty badass. That he told me that? I mean Brandon had all this shit going on in his own head nobody knew about. He didn't want to talk about him; he'd want to talk about being happy for *you*."

"There are a thousand stories I could tell: like the first football game from last year, Brandon rode over here with some friends. Jamy and Brandon were sitting in the front seat. Jamy tried to get in the car and they'd pulled off and drive up the road a little bit. They kept taking off and stopping and not letting him in. It was funny as hell. And you know, right, why Brandon Moore enlisted in the Marines? Ladner talked him into it."

"They came over here that Friday night and all of us decided to go over to Johnny Cosby's house (another Marine). The car was dangerous to drive, I mean the wheels were about to fall off. The bearings were about to go out and we told Moore, 'Moore, this ain't good. We're going to end up driving straight into that truck.' So we all put on our seatbelts. Everybody was laughing so hard. We were driving along and the sound coming from the front tires was exactly like you hear on a rollercoaster as it's going up for its first drop, 'Click, click, click.'

"Of course, it being two in the morning, we were all drunk. The click, click, click started up again and Brandon suddenly lifted his arms up like he was riding a roller coaster. We all started laughing so damn hard. Moore had no idea what we were laughing about which made it that much funnier. We couldn't make fun of Brandon Moore though because he couldn't buy a new car. His was a real piece of work, and we weren't sure we were going to make it home." Mr. Hodges paused. "It was the funniest shit in the world. Moore kept asking what we were all laughing about but we couldn't tell him his car sucked, right? Brandon did shit like that all the time. He kept everybody laughing."

"The way I learned about Brandon's passing went like this. My wife works with Brandon Moore who'd found out what happened. He found out, shared with my wife who then called me. I was at work on this big conference call. She called to tell me and I just had to leave. Four or five people met me at the man cave and all of us just sat there together drinking and crying for Brandon."

"That night I was sitting in the cave all by myself, the place my buddy Brandon loved. I was sitting there with the garage door open thinking, 'Brandon, if you're here, show me.' Now, I'm no kind of ghost hunter by any means but I have to share this. The light on my garage door came on. I didn't know what to think about that. Maybe it was nothing, maybe it was just a coincidence. Maybe it was selfish of me to want him to be there. I just wish things hadn't happened like they did with Brandon."

"The next weekend, everybody was in the cave watching the game and I was thinking how everybody would be going home after the night was over, everybody except for Brandon. If he was still with us, I knew he'd be here the next day. Brandon would be up and happy, even with a hangover, helping clean the place up, take the trash out. He was always so happy, and I was happy he was there too."

"I had two buddies in the cave and we'd all been watching football from ten that morning all the way until midnight. It was a long damn time to be drinking. I was telling my buddies about the light, telling them what I'd said to Brandon, 'I love you man, show me you're here' and you know what happened? The light turned off. Maybe it was Brandon, or again, I read into it too much into it, but it was a hell of a damn time for it to be a coincidence. That was pretty amazing shit and everybody was floored that it happened."

"There was another time, Brandon and I were sitting at his mom's house. I was running with Chris, (Brandon's brother) and his mom didn't get a chance to meet me. I was in college and three years older than Brandon but admired the fact that he was so wise for his age. He was just so determined. I mean, he had a plan and was determined to follow that plan no matter what. He got it in his head that he wanted to be a Marine and he was going to do whatever it took to become one. I was in this law class and had no idea what I wanted to do with my life. He was this sixteen year old, more mature than I was at the time. I knew he was one of the good guys who'd be there and do the right thing. But make no mistake; if somebody got sideways, he'd take care of that too."

"I wanted a friend who'd have my back, and Brandon was the one: no doubt about it. He never tried to be anybody that he wasn't. For instance, if anybody wanted to try starting something with him, he'd try talking that person out of making an issue. He'd say something like, 'That's probably not a good idea." We'd do dumb-ass guy shit too, and arm wrestle all the time. He'd let you use two arms to his one and he'd still move your entire body Brandon was strong as shit, like the damn Hulk."

"He was somebody special. I respected him so much. I mean, there I was in college, and he was still in high school. I respected the hell out of him because of how worldly mature and wise he was for only being 16. He was thinking about the Corps and talking about retiring in twenty-five years. I wasn't thinking about any of that retirement shit and I was older than he was. He was something else."

☐

-Chris Espey, USMC-

"Brandon always wanted more out of life. He worked more than he played."

Before Chris Espey considered sharing this interview, the soft-spoken Marine Veteran did a lot of thinking. When it came right down to the matter of answering the same set of questions that were being posed to everyone else, Mr. Espey initially chose to submit written responses, but a hesitant phone call soon followed.

"The first time I ever met Brandon was at one of the local pubs in town. I was with a fellow Veteran, Millard Downey, who, by the way was a great lifelong friend of Brandon's. He sought out to introduce the two of us because Brandon was a fellow Marine. We immediately hit it off and, as all Vets tend to do, started exchanging units, MOS's, telling a few short stories about our own deployments and the places we had each been. I remember instantly finding out that we had a few things in common, one being that we never boasted or tried to 'one up' each other like some vets have the tendency to do. It was just simple small talk really, but we were both so enthused to meet a fellow hometown vet especially since we were the same and had mutual friends."

"Speaking for myself, I felt a little withdrawn from the rest of society and have always been a bit hesitant in meeting people. When Ladner and I met, it was a big relief to not experience those feelings of anxiety. After a few hours of playing pool and just hanging out with other friends, we began talking more openly about our feelings regarding deployments, people, and just everything in general. I dare say that he and I established a bond almost instantly, realizing that we both had a lot of the same views about life after the military."

"Brandon was a person you'd easily take notice of, even in a room full of people. He was one of those guys who always had this huge smile on his face. He always wore nice clothes everywhere, even on random mud riding sessions or hanging out by a bonfire. He was the big, jacked-up guy in the corner who dressed nice and liked to cut up with his friends. It didn't matter if you were a stranger, as you'd get to know him, you'd easily hear it in his voice that he was a lighthearted kind of guy and had an amusing tone in his voice as he spoke, no matter the topic at hand. It was the kind of tone where you'd think, 'This guy can't possibly be serious about anything,' but once you got to know him, you knew exactly what he was all about."

"Like most friends in our group, Brandon always had your back, no matter what the situation. If anyone needed anything, he'd always help with whatever he had or could do. Having met other Marine brothers of his, I learned that he had carried that same outlook in the military and he was known throughout the service. Brandon always wanted more out of life and was the type who worked harder than he played."

"I wish I had more stories to tell about him, but I only knew him for little over a year before he passed. I can share this though; our endeavors essentially involved hanging out with our group of friends, just drinking and having good times and talking about life in general. I usually sat back and listened to all the stuff he talked about and laughed right along with everyone else. Those were some good times."

"The way I found out about what happened to Brandon was via text from Ashley. I immediately called to check on her and asked if anyone else knew yet. I know this may sound odd, but I was kind of numb when it came to receiving news about losing friends at that point, having already lost four other friends to suicide that same year. Ashley told me that she didn't think anyone else knew at that point. I immediately called our friend Millard and remember the conversation going something like this:

"What's up, Brother?" he answered. I responded with a simple, 'Not much, man. Are you driving right now or at home?' "At home, why? What happened now?"

"We'd shared these calls before with each other and later, Millard told me that he'd heard it in my voice. He already knew that another brother had died but never expected it to be one he knew personally this time. I shared the news about Brandon, and there were probably three minutes of complete silence."

"I know, brother. I'm heading your way right now."

The soft and quiet demeanor in Chris's voice had already contradicted the picture I had formed in my mind. Marines are supposed to be rough and tough and are as loud as they are proud. It was apparent that this Marine had put much thought into the next words he shared. "I knew a lot about Mission22 before this all happened with Brandon. About a month before his death, I'd lost another great brother whom I served with personally. It felt like this was becoming an epidemic."

"My personal view about suicide hasn't changed. The people who say it's a cowardly act or the same ones who sit back and shrug their shoulders and ask 'why?' They've obviously never been pushed to that point in their lives. It's a real struggle. I think about it: daily. I've taken a few serious, close attempts to end my own life, only to have been rescued by things I can't explain. I still zone out, lay awake at night and wonder when the next call will come. Who's it going to be? Will it be me?"

"I've learned to realize that when I get to that point and start thinking along those lines, it's time to call my brothers or go hang out with them. They don't know what thoughts are going through my head at the time; they just know that I want to hang out. It's a constant battle to push those thoughts away but it's a lot easier to do when you're with other people. PTSD is a demon that's strongest when it's got you alone."

"My transition after the military was a pretty rough process. In the beginning, I carried a lot of anger with no sense of hope. I went from being a sergeant in the Marines to low man on the totem pole. I had to realize I was dealing with a whole different world. I'd grown used to seeing the world from the military point of view, a view so different than what I'd left back home. I came home and looked at people around me and was like, 'What are y'all doing with your lives?' You grow up quick when you go to war. People back home have all the opportunities in the world but they throw that away. I was on my first deployment at the age of nineteen. When I turned twenty-one, I was still on deployment. By the age of twenty-two, all of that was gone."

"I'd achieved all the goals I had planned for my life by the time I turned twenty-one. When I came back home, I had to start back at the bottom. I'd wanted the career but was pushed out for PTSD that was caused by the very job I had been trained to do. I'd just gone through a divorce a few months before my discharge, was fresh out of rehab and three months sober. Coming home was difficult because my life had changed so much in such a short span of time. In the year prior to all that, I still had a career, a wife, and child waiting for me at home. It's easy to see how such changes in life can drive a person to think about certain things; drive a person to do certain things."

"I felt like the last three years of my life were a complete waste of time. I spent it wandering around drinking, trying to sort my life out in totally the wrong way. Right now, I'm in a completely new atmosphere. I've moved, started school and well, there's no temptation. I can say this new perspective saved my life. It's still hard sometimes because I don't have all the friends here that I did back in my hometown. Back there, whenever anything was wrong, all I had to do was call and they'd be there. Living here, all I have are calls. A lot can happen in a three-hour drive to a brother's house, knowing what's on his mind."

"I've slowly but surely realized my potential. I have newfound goals in my life that I strive to reach every day. The nights are still something I struggle with, but I lay down each night with the goal to see daylight the next morning and go from there. For me, it's one day at a time, one phone call at a time. Eventually, I'll figure out how to space all that out and live a somewhat normal life. I know one thing for sure; you have to crawl before you can walk."

☐

-Tyler 'Debo' Lumpkin-
"I wished I'd known he was feeling like that."

"Brandon Ladner was always a happy-go-lucky kind of guy, always had a big ole smile on his face. His wasn't your regular kind of smile, either. Brandon would smile with his whole face and showed you exactly how he felt," Mr. Lumpkin paused before adding, "-and he laughed a lot. Brandon sort of had a chuckle to his laugh. If you were having an off-day, you'd feel better after he came around. He always seemed to let things slide off his own shoulders pretty easily. I never knew him to want to go get in a fight with anybody just because he was mad at them or anything."

"As an adult, I didn't see Brandon often. I'd moved away and would still come around, but not often. Back when we were kids, I was more friends with his older brother Chris, who was closer to my age than Brandon was. Brandon didn't hang out with us too much back then, though. He had his own group of friends. It's hard to remember those days, you know?"

Mr. Lumpkin drew in a slow breath as he thought about his next words. "When I first found out about Brandon, I was totally shocked. Like I said, I'd moved away from the old neighborhood and hadn't seen too much of him. The thing is though, I'd run into him about seven or eight months prior, and we'd went out to a few bars in Pelham. (Hodges was there, too and so was his wife.) I remember we were all just laughing it up and having a good time by the end of that night. We were all hanging right after I'd broken up with a girl, broke my own heart. It was nice to hang out and be able to talk about things."

"Brandon was the second person I'd known who left this world like that. It was that previous January that we had all been hanging out, drinking and having a good time when he and I ended up out on the back porch just shootin' the breeze. We were drinking some shine and talking about how good he was doing, and there I was, sitting around moping because of the whole break-up with my girlfriend deal. He stood there and told me I needed to get my mind off stuff." Tyler paused. "He helped a lot."

"When I found out what happened to Brandon, my first thought was something like, 'I wish I'd known he was feeling like that.' When I started seeing 'rest in peace' messages all over Facebook, and stuff on the feeds, I clicked on his name, went to his page and was all like, 'Woe.' When I saw his mama posting on there, I knew it was real. As for the statistic 'twenty-two a day,' I didn't know what that meant until it was explained to me."

"I hadn't seen him since that January, but to me, there weren't any signs that he was having problems. I know what a difference just a few months can make though, when the walls start feeling like they're closing in on you, something is going to give."

□

-Heather Hartfield-

"I hope wherever he is, Brandon can see what an impact he led, had on other people's lives."

"I first met Brandon when we were students at Thompson High School. We had an English class together. He and I immediately connected and became really good friends. Brandon was the light in the classroom, always making everybody laugh."

"How would I describe him?" The string of words came easily for Mrs. Hartfield. "Funny, kind, extremely out-going, handsome, and always the life of the party."

"Brandon was a very loyal and kind person. He never turned his back on a friend and was *always* there if you needed him, even for people who didn't think to do the same for him. He always placed other people before himself, even serving his country. Brandon was selfless, but you know, sometimes we, as humans need to be selfish; just a little bit. I think that him being so selfless was almost a fault. He always put his needs on the back burner."

"I'll never forget one of the last conversations we had with him. My husband, Brandon and I were all sitting out on our back porch. We were out there just visiting and having a good time when Brandon turned all serious and was like, 'Man, you two have it together. I want that.' We told him, 'Listen. You have the potential to do whatever you want to do, be whatever you want to be and love whoever you want to love.' I'll always remember that conversation because it my heart. That was the first time I ever saw that side of Brandon. When he opened up to us, it was both humbling and heartbreaking at the same time. It made me appreciate more the things that we all tend to take for granted in our everyday lives."

"When I first found out the news about Brandon, I was at work. I had called Amy Winslett, a classmate of ours (and friend of

Brandon's girlfriend at the time) to ask her a question about some other matter. Amy didn't answer the phone, but her boss did. She told me that Amy had left work because one of her friends had suddenly passed away. I managed to get a hold of her, but when I got Amy on the phone, she was hysterical. She told me what happened and then I told my boss and left work."

"I was kind of in shock for a while. It was completely unexpected, more along the lines of unbelievable to be quite honest with you. I called my husband to tell him what had happened and reacted in kind of the same way. He made me repeat myself and was all like, 'What are you talking about?' For the rest of that day, Brandon was on my mind. I had to tell other friends about what had happened, not an easy call to make. It was a difficult time."

"Twenty-two a day: I knew about this statistic. My sister and her boyfriend wrote, directed, and starred in a short film about a female Marine who'd been a part of a Marine female engagement team in Afghanistan who was suffering from PTSD. Their film has won numerous awards, so I knew what twenty-two was about before everything happened with Brandon."

"I don't know how to put this into words. If I had the opportunity, I wish I could talk to Brandon. I would assure him that everything was going to be okay and that he had people who loved him that he could talk to any of us. We didn't know the warning signs or what to do to help him. I guess we saw the changes but didn't know exactly what we were seeing."

"Something changes in you when you become a mother, and I feel for Ms. Renee. If I had to bury my own son, well, it's just so heartbreaking, such a horrible thing that no mother should ever have to do. I pray that she knows how truly loved Brandon was. I can understand how some people can't talk about losing him from their life. People may not be ready for that yet."

"I hope wherever he is, Brandon can see what an impact he led, had on other people's lives. My friends and I still talk about him all the time. We just had our 10th-year class reunion, and Brandon is one of six from our class who are no longer with us because of various reasons. All of us are still here, but six of our classmates don't get to have that. It was such an eye-opener. We tend to take our daily lives for granted, at least until we sit down and see who doesn't have what we consider so given."

☐

-Tyler Orr-

"He was always like a brother to me."

"One of my favorite memories of Brandon is from high school when we all used to ride dirt bikes together. One day, for some reason or another, I wasn't able to go out riding with him. In the days before either of us had our driver's license, we used to ride on all the trails that connected the neighborhoods in Alabaster together so it was easy for us to get to each other's houses. On that particular day, I received this call from Brandon. 'I know you're not home, but don't freak out when you do come in and see my dirt bike in your garage. The Game Warden chased me on the trails, but I lost him in your neighborhood so I left my bike in your garage. If he shows up looking for me, I'm already gone.' It wasn't twenty minutes later that my mom called me wanting to know why the Game Warden was at the house looking for a kid on a dirt bike. I explained to her what was going on and so she went out to the Warden and said 'No sir. I haven't seen anyone around here on a dirt bike. My son isn't even here but his bike is in the garage. Good luck finding whoever you're looking for.' That is my most treasured memory of Brandon. He was always like a brother to me growing up and my family loved him like he was my brother."

☐

-Rachel Slaughter-Foster -

"Brandon proudly served with every ounce of being: heart and soul."

"I was taking care of my grandfather (who was also a Veteran, by the way) about five years ago and we had decided to go to one of the local state parks to have a cook out. I think it was back sometime around 2010 or 2011 at Oak Mountain. I first meet Brandon back around the same time. I'll never forget it, either. I remember thinking to myself how tremendously good-looking he was." Rachel smiled.

"If you were in the same room as Brandon, he'd be easy to spot. He'd be the guy making everybody laugh. Brandon was the type of man that people would radiate to. As I said before, he was a damn fine-looking Marine who seemed to have everything going for him. He was good-looking, sweet, kind, and knew how to treat a lady. He had such a beautiful smile and was so generous with his hugs. They were genuine 'I care about you' hugs, too. You never heard of him being anything but good to people: all people."

"One memorable thing I can tell you about Brandon (and there are so many) is the way he could so easily make you feel better about yourself even when you were feeling low or depressed. I was going through some things at one point and was feeling pretty bad all the way around. Here comes Brandon with one of his big bear hugs. He just stepped up, hugged me and started talking, telling me all kinds of positive things and being so encouraging and sweet." Rachel paused as tears glistened in her eyes, "You just don't meet that kind of person in this world anymore; not like him."

"I remember one cookout we had at the house. It was a nice little get-together, even Nicole and her husband were there. My son had decided to start shouting out all kinds of obscenities throughout the neighborhood. There was no doubt that he was acting a little 'off' that day but Brandon, who by the way was the chef that day, stopped what he was doing and went to talk with my son who was just in absolute awe of Brandon. He calmed him down without any problem. He admired Brandon."

"When I heard about what had happened, my first thought was 'How could Brandon leave his mom and family?' I thought he had everything so perfect in his life, and from what everybody could see, it was, but it's not all about the stuff on the outside. I guess everything we saw, well, how he saw his own life was different than what the rest of us saw. He was a beautiful man, had a good job, seemed to have exactly what he wanted in life and was working on reaching all the goals he had set for himself."

"I don't know what to say about that number twenty-two. I think Brandon was who he was but believed he had to be so strong, that he had to deal with things by himself but that wasn't true. He had so many people he could talk to. When everything happened, and I started hearing that number get thrown around, I didn't understand it at first. It was so incomprehensible to me. I still can't understand it. Well, yes I can. I can only imagine how Brandon must have been feeling. Like I keep saying, he had a good job, a roof over his head, people to come home to, to surround himself with." Rachel paused as she shook her head. "We need to do more to help those dealing with PTSD. I would have never guessed Brandon to be one who'd do that. It was such a shock. I guess we'll never know for sure why."

"Brandon proudly served his country with every ounce of being: heart and soul. He had to travel away from all his friends and family for several deployments but we were all lucky: he was one of the ones who came home. I have this image in my mind of how he served." Rachel sat back in her chair as she paused to catch her thoughts. "He was over there helping to keep all that from coming over here; he helped to protect the rest of us. He was the sweetest soul you could have ever met." As she wrapped up her interview session, Rachel Slaughter-Foster smiled and gave a little laugh. "Roll Tide, roll! We love you Brandon, and you'll always be in our hearts."

☐

-Breaze Humphries-
"He was very comforting and had such a good heart."

"It's a little complicated describing how Brandon became part of my life. When I was ten years old (and he was eight) Brandon, Nicole and their brother Chris moved to Pelham from Mississippi. My dad (Bob) and mom had recently divorced, so their mom and my dad ended up hitting it off and started dating. It all worked out though because Brandon and my younger brother Beau ended up being in the same grade. Brandon's sister Nicole and I were in the same grade ahead of them. Renee, my dad, and all us kids meshed well together."

When asked to describe Brandon, Breaze had to give the matter some thought. "There are so many words. I have to think about this a minute." However, after some deep contemplating, the words came easily. "Happy, bubbly, fun. Brandon was always the guy who could lift everybody up. He had such a great smile and would give the most terrific bear hugs. I don't remember ever seeing him in a bad mood: ever."

"Name one particularly outstanding quality about Brandon? He was attentive: a good listener. He was somebody who paid attention to everything you'd say. It was almost like when you told him something, he could easily relate to whatever your problem was. He was comforting and had such a good heart. I'm not trying to talk him up or anything; that's just who he was. He was one of those people who was so easy to get along with."

"I'd moved to North Carolina when I was younger so I only had a few years to spend with Brandon. The best memories I have with him, though, are ones we made after we were both adults. He'd gotten out of the Corps and would come over to the house all the time to do yard work, or for dinner and drinks, play pool or whatever. Brandon looked up to my dad."

"I have a lot of fun memories with Brandon, but here's one I remember particularly. I'd moved back in with my dad right before my daughter was born. Brandon came over for one of his regular visits, and as you know, he was a big 'Bama fan. I remember one night, he asked me my opinion about what did I think about what if Auburn and Alabama ever played each other in a SEC game. That's when I had to explain the rules to him, about how both teams were in the Western division and that they'd never play against one another. He took it all in stride. *"I can't believe a girl knows more about football than me."* That's a good memory to me because it was so funny. He was only two years younger than I, but that's one of the last fun memories we shared. That was a good time."

"It's kind of hard to talk about when I first found out what happened. On the morning of September 9th, I'd already been awake since around five a.m. after I'd received a call about my last grandparent who had just passed away. I had to go to work for about an hour first, but I'd already planned to take the rest of the day off to deal with his passing. I did what I needed to do at the office and was headed for the house when I received a call from his Aunt Laurie. "Brandon's gone," and she told me what happened. I lost it, I mean, I really lost it. I sat there on the side of the road and cried for thirty minutes before pulling myself together enough to make it to my dad's."

"Pawpaw was 91 years old: his death was kind of expected. Brandon was only two years younger than me. I couldn't believe it. My first thoughts were that it all had to be a dream, that it hadn't happened. I went to my grandfather's funeral and then the next day I went to Brandon's. It was so sad. I couldn't believe it. The last time we were together we'd been drinking beer on dad's porch and talking about football."

"Twenty-two a day. I think the reason that number is so unstable, (and I've never been in their shoes) because," Mrs. Humphries paused before she continued. "-well, I think if I ever had to experience the things that so many of our guys had to go through over there, I guess part of that would continue to sit uneasy with me, too. I think this has made coming home and adjusting back to the lives they left behind hard for our guys today. The whole war experience is going to weigh on their minds and in their hearts every day. I think the way the world turns and how crazy everything seems to be today is just so heartbreaking. Our guys come home, but they can't escape the war. They can't completely turn it off."

"We are such a plugged-in world today. People go to war; they come home and think, 'Okay. I'm done. It's over,' but yet, the television or the computer or feeds on their smartphones are still posting news about Isis or articles about service members getting killed by roadside bombs, random attacks and they have nowhere to go to escape that. They're still hearing about what's happening over there on the news every day even after they come back home." Mrs. Humphries paused and took a deep breath. "I don't know what can be done to help them, but I can see how it's so difficult for them to 'come back.' It doesn't seem like it's getting any better."

"Brandon was always a happy guy. I can remember times with every one of my other siblings where I had to 'be there' for them, help them through some rough spot or another, but never with Brandon. He was always happy. This may sound funny but when I think of him, I remember his teeth because he was always smiling, always so in-tune with what I was talking about. Brandon was like that with whoever he'd be talking to with whatever you were talking about. He'd always let me just talk and talk and talk and would never interrupt. He'd sit there and listen, taking it all in and then he'd give me feedback if I wanted it. Brandon was just that kind of guy."

☐

-Bob Lipsey-

"I'd talked to him a million times…but I couldn't reach him."

On the evening of June 11th, several hours following the special Honor and Remember Flag Presentation in Montevallo, Alabama an unexpected interview happened to occur. Mr. Bob Lipsey, Brandon's step-father agreed to give a few minutes of his time and sat with author Fitzgerald in the living room of Brandon's former childhood home. The house was full of people and laughter as friends and family socialized. No doubt about it, it seemed pretty evident that everyone was having a good time. Laughter could be heard in the background as Mr. Lipsey settled in to give his interview. "I'm an extremely difficult person to get a hold of." He commented he sat down in the spacious living room.

The first question asked from the standard set of interview questions seemed peculiar as Fitzgerald asked Mr. Lipsey how he had first met Brandon. After a lot of deep thought and consideration, Mr. Lipsey simply conveyed, "Brandon and my son Beau were compadres." Mr. Lipsey took a breath as he smiled. "That's the first time I ever met Brandon. The boys were about eight years old. I was divorced, his mom was divorced, my daughter and Brandon's sister got along well and they acted as matchmakers for Renee and me."

As with each other interview that had been taken, when Mr. Lipsey was asked for adjectives he would use in describing his step-son, he didn't have to think long at all, as he immediately shared the words that came so easily to mind, "Brandon was always on the go. He was upfront, active, and definitely not bashful. He was a great kid with a great personality." Appearing satisfied with his answer, Mr. Lipsey sat back. Seeming a little more at ease with the whole interview process, he softly added, "Brandon's empathy and compassion for others were also great traits."

"When I first heard what had happened to Brandon, I felt empty and shocked," Mr. Lipsey took a moment to compose his next thought. "-but not surprised. There'd been indications. I'd commented to my wife Barbara that I was concerned about him. I had concerns but never thought Brandon had it in himself to end his life. I had just talked with him the night before." The emotion had grown audibly heavier in Mr. Lipsey's voice. "When I heard the news, I felt totally empty."

"After Brandon got out of the Marines, I don't think he processed back into civilian life very well. He'd come over here and want to talk, and I could tell there was something heavy on his mind. I could see a lot of emptiness in his eyes. Brandon felt a lot of guilt and remorse for the men he had served with who'd been killed in action. He couldn't shake that. I talked to him a million times about it but couldn't ever seem to reach him. He had it in his mind that he should have never made it back, that he should have been one of those guys."

Despite his easy-going demeanor, Mr. Lipsey's emotions betrayed him. It was apparent how much he loved and missed Brandon. Mr. Lipsey thoughtfully answered every question presented to him, giving each answer a tremendous amount of consideration before sharing his thoughts. "Brandon was," Bob Lipsey paused. "-the world missed out on a bright young man that had so much talent." It seemed as if Mr. Lipsey was searching for just the right words to say next. "You know, talent can be used to help people, and Brandon? Brandon had so much, but he wasted his."

"Brandon was always offering to help my wife and I here around the house. He'd come over, cut the grass or tend to the pool, whatever needed to be done. He was always helping out." Mr. Lipsey stared up at the ceiling for a moment before finishing his interview. When he spoke, tears filled his eyes as a quietly conveyed, "In this day and time where young people don't care about anything, don't care about life, Brandon cared. He genuinely cared about his family. He loved us all." Nodding his head toward the doorway as a burst of laughter made its way from the kitchen, Bob commented with a smile. "That's how Brandon would have wanted things: laughter and everybody having a good time."

□ -Sometimes Marines Cry-

T-M Fitzgerald

12/30/2013

(Originally written July 29, 2012, this piece has also appeared previously in another Fitzgerald work 'From Yellow Ribbons to a Gold Star') It seemed especially appropriate to share with Brandon's story.

Holding the last drag as long as his lungs would let him,
He finished his final cigarette and abruptly excused himself.

Mysterious, yet so serious,
And only he could tell you why-
Too frequently left to his own devices,
He swore, "They'll never see me cry."

Too often he'd startle awake at night,
Pulling thoughts from out of the air-
"How would anyone find me?" he'd think,
Then stare blankly to the empty chair.

People'd kindly ask, "What's wrong?"
Then dare to comment, "You shouldn't dwell."
None of them had any way of knowing,
How or why his life had become such hell.

He'd sit there alone, lost deep in thought,
Searching the depths of his soul,
Debating his life for one more night,
Imagining how his story would get told.

He thought of lost friends as lumps filled his throat-
And hot tears welled up in his eyes.
The things he still saw, did not want to see,
And had long since learned to despise.

He tried catching those shooting stars,
Wishing hard as each one tumbled from the sky.
He'd look down into his still, two empty hands,
And then thought to ask himself, "Why?"

He worried little about dying,
And one day just locked the door.
Wasn't worried today, he'd made the decision;
He wasn't going back to 'that place' anymore.

The people in those glass houses there?
He wished they'd stop throwin' their stones.
And if nobody meant it when they 'offered a hand?'
Then he'd prefer to be just left alone.

It'd all be over soon enough,
If the fat lady would just shut up and sing-
But each day, he'd wait and each day would retire,
Without hearing a solitary thing.

And the knife throwing guy? He saw him, there too-
In the shadows over by the door.
That guy who's blind? Well, he's fake, too
And doesn't need to come by here anymore.

His journey soon began where others' had ended,
Events well beyond anyone's comprehension.
He couldn't believe, couldn't fathom the things-
The many factors everyone had failed to mention.

So he got sent back home,
With more guilt than he'd known-
(And you know? The crazy bitch never did sing.)
He quit all his frettin'
Began years of regrettin',
His only satisfaction was with knowing that he'd tried.

It was then,
And only then
That the Marine took pause…
Slowly sat down …
And cried.

☐

-No Knock on the Door-
"To the shores of Tripoli: almost."

It seems an easy enough task for anybody to sit down and write a book. After all, a person needs only to find the right motivation, have the desire or drive, choose a starting point (wherever that particular point may be) and begin. After completing many rounds of meticulous research and taking in-depth interviews with numerous people, work on writing everything down in an engaging enough manner that will move people to read more than two or three pages in a single sitting. Writing a book: pretty simple, or so it would seem. That was not the case here.

First and foremost, *From Motorcycles to Machine Guns* was put together as a biographical account about one specific Marine; not a number, not a statistic, but a Marine. His name was Brandon Charles Ladner, sergeant in the United States Marine Corps. In reading his story, do not misunderstand the purposeful nonexistence of all-encompassing terminology or politically correct phrasing as anything other than what it is. The focus was Brandon, the intent was to introduce *him* and share *his* story with the rest of the world.

It was expressed by numerous individuals how Brandon loved people: so much to the point that it's also been said that he never knew a stranger. However, pulling Brandon's story together was a particularly challenging task as many of those who knew and lived by him were extremely hesitant to speak out. It proved difficult for many to step forward and talk about the tragic and unexpected loss of a man who, from all outward appearances appeared to have had the world by the tail.

"Brandon touched so many of us. Our lives are forever changed because we were a part of his. He was so hilarious and genuine. He would go out of his way for people and stand for what he believed in. He was a beautiful soul and the world is truly darker since his light has burned out. PTSD is a REAL killer. Wars don't end in the minds of the heroes."

-Jessica Barnes

"Just because Brandon isn't here, know this; he's still making a difference and changing lives."

-Brandi Lavender

Compiling Brandon's story turned out to be a testament to just how rough acknowledgment and acceptance of his death and the manner in which it happened has been to so many. Despite the potential difficulties faced in pulling this Marine's story together, the author was determined to pursue and assemble something on a personal level, safeguarding and preserving Brandon's memory so that future generations could know him.

For any writer of non-fiction, it is vital, paramount to give every project one hundred percent effort and care. When writing about the military, that fact is particularly important, often necessitating a 'one hundred ten percent and beyond' standard. Brandon Ladner's was not the first story this author has written about a Marine. In writing those earlier books and stories, author Fitzgerald, herself a Veteran of the United States Army, had to complete tremendous research. Imagine that: an Army Veteran writing about Marines; every 'T' had to be crossed and every 'i' dotted along the way, and not just any way. Things had to be done the Marine way.

In researching, reading, and talking about United States Marines, numerous facts have been spoken as well as written which are continuously being repeated. It's because of that fact that it stands to reason when applying the 'one hundred and ten percent' standard to the task of writing about yet another outstanding young Marine, many comments, statements, and facts may seem repetitive, perhaps even vaguely familiar to readers and fans of military-themed literature. This is not due to any lack of determination or study.

It is an honor to write about such men, those who've made up the various components of the all-volunteer force that like it or not, help keep America safe. It's important to note though, that despite the tragic way his life concluded, the story of this Marine began long before those familiar words, "*I, Brandon Charles Ladner do solemnly swear that I will support and defend the Constitution of the United States against all enemies foreign and domestic...*"

And such men? This is a story written about an enlisted man who chose to step up and defend his country. It wasn't a biography about some revered general or elite commander who somehow accomplished a seemingly impossible task against insurmountable odds. This was the story of a highly regarded man who survived serving his country abroad but lost his personal battle with a demon at home: PTSD, the same demon that has created a crack, which over the course of generations, too many have fallen into. Like the Titan named Atlas, Brandon Ladner, a United States Marine, found himself with the weight of the world on his shoulders. This was the ultimate reason why Brandon's story was such a necessary one needing to be told.

The loss of this Marine touched upon a very sensitive topic. Brandon actively served during Operation Enduring Freedom (OEF) where thousands of men before him had already been KIA: killed in action in country. He returned home to Alabama, another fortunate warrior who had served in a questionable war. He'd never faltered, never failed; never questioned the commands or duties that fell his way. Brandon was one of those men who tried making everybody's time in-country (overseas) a little more bearable in the best way he knew how: with humor. He came home, but not as the same man who had left.

Though some may refute this fact, the loss of Brandon Ladner's life in Alabama was no different than the loss of a Marine killed overseas. Any loss of life is an ugly part of war no matter where in the scheme of events it occurs. Brandon's story may feel like a familiar one and on several levels, it should. His story just happened in a different place, in a different time but keep in mind also the fact that this was *his* story.

With his death, Ladner brought much-needed attention to a particularly sad, controversial and subjective statistic. Brandon was not one of the thousands killed in action (KIA) overseas following 9-11: quite the contrary. Instead, this young Marine sergeant safely returned stateside after deployment to Afghanistan only to end up as one of the thousands who've taken their own life in a war 'over here'. (Because that's what it is, you know: another war, a war at home.) On September 09, 2014 Brandon took his own life in-country, this country, in his own home. As painful a fact that is to see in print, it became Ladner's mother's hope that by sharing Brandon's story and raising awareness about the demon that took her son, it might help to save another's life.

Tragically, Ladner's story became one of many that needed to be told long after everybody thought the war 'over there' had ended. In 2015, studies were published supporting the fact that since the beginning of the 'War on Terrorism,' the number of Veteran suicides had surpassed the number of casualties incurred in battle. There are people who claim the media has that information all wrong, that it's purposefully misleading the public, diverting the mass's attention away from things going on elsewhere in the government. (Tell that to those who've lost a child, a brother, a sister or friend. Tell all *those* people it doesn't happen like that and ask them what they think or know about that 'misleading' statistic.)

☐ First, here is something to think about: why should members of a non-military public (i.e. civilians) feel obligated to read stories and articles written about the United States military? Maybe more to the point, why should anybody care to read anything written about Veterans who have taken their own lives? The answer to that question is quite simple; because this is your country, one currently protected by a less than 10% of the population, an all-volunteer force by the way: 24/7-365 (or in other words, twenty-four hours a day, three hundred sixty-five days a year). However, if that answer doesn't satisfy you, here's one more point to consider; what is it that goes so wrong that causes multiple Veterans from the same deployment to take their own lives in rapid succession? How is it that no measurable progress has been made to solve the problem? THAT is why other people/civilians should feel compelled to read stories about the military: their military.

If people think they don't need to take the time to care, then consider what the future of this country could realistically become. It's easy enough to look at and observe the horrors taking place in other countries and convince oneself that 'nothing like that could ever happen in this country' because so far, nothing has; but consider the reason why: our military. If nobody cares today, what will the future of the USA be tomorrow?

This book addressed the current battle that too many of our Veterans are still fighting. Nobody likes the 's' word, but Veterans across generations are still in conflict with ghosts that nobody else can see. Too many are continuing to lose personal battles with PTSD, and the end result has become a sobering statistic: 22/day. That's twenty-two Veterans a day choosing to take their own lives by suicide.

Though written about a solitary man, *From Motorcycles to Machine Guns* was written and deemed to be shared as a necessary step in raising awareness about a problem affecting a much larger population. Remembering this Marine is one step in a direction we all need to go. Perhaps by bringing attention to Brandon Ladner's story, we will accomplish what his mother hopes and another's life can be saved.

☐ In his book, *The Invisible Front: Love and Loss in an Era of Endless War,* Author Yochi Dreazen wrote *"Depression and traumatic stress are seen as signs of weakness in the military world. Stigma keeps warriors from seeking help."* Dreazen further wrote how in the year 2014, the Pentagon revealed the suicide rate for Veterans aged 30 and younger had jumped 44% between 2009 and 2011. War continued taking a psychological toll. "Suicide is the military's newest war."

"September 09th, 2014. A day that began like any other: for *most* people. September 09th was the day one more Marine mother became the recipient of unwanted gold. For the 1st Battalion, 5th Division, Sgt. Brandon Ladner was not the first Marine who unexplainably felt compelled to take his own life. (Nor, sadly enough, was he the last.) It's not necessary to know exactly where in the order of so many heart-wrenching losses that Brandon made his own tragic decision. Instead, what was deemed extremely necessary was the sharing of his life. For thousands of soldiers and Marines deployed to Afghanistan to defend this country, many never got to come home, were never able to tell their own stories. For thousands more, (like Brandon) the war 'over there' inevitably killed them over here. Their stories still needed to be told."

In a world in serious need of heroes, we almost expect those elaborate, ghost-written stories of generals and kings. You know the ones: *"How I Won the Battle of_____," "The Life Story of General____."* The book you hold in your hand has been the tale of a warrior no less great, a United States Marine who willfully stepped forward to fight on behalf of his country, but one who did not make it all the way home when his tour was complete. This book personifies a man who the entire world would liked to have known. It's the story of a man who uniquely touched the lives of countless others but whose own life took an unexpected turn long before September 09, 2014.

The idea for Brandon's book began (September 09, 2014) as that statistic '22 a day' reared its ugly head yet again in a seemingly constant series of incidents. Shortly following, word was put out that I wanted to contact Brandon's mother Renee. Cole Wilson, fellow 1/5 Marine immediately touched base with her and forwarded my information. I'd respectfully waited a year before making any approach. Brandon's mother Renee and I eventually connected and ended up chatting on the phone until a little after two the morning on October 03rd, 2015. Commencement of *From Motorcycles to Machine Guns* happened two weeks later.

Service members who've fought together tend to be very protective of one another, no matter when or where they served, no matter if they're living or gone from this world. Memory matters and the brotherhood of the Marines in particular, exemplifies this fact. It wasn't just his fellow Marines, though whose lives Ladner touched so deeply. It wasn't just fellow Marines who continued to protect his memory.

It was a peculiar feeling to scroll through different pages, posts, and pictures all across different social media venues, almost intrusive, as if I were looking through some private keyhole into the life of this Marine. There came many questions, many thoughts and tremendous wondering whether or not I'd get people to open up. Would I be able to learn enough about him to write an entire book? I knew his was a story needing to be told, no matter what. Besides, I'd made a promise and am a Veteran of my word.

Every person's life is defined by specific moments. This book was about some of Brandon's. The goal was to make it easier for people to feel okay about sitting down and sharing his story for the rest of the world to read. The following has been mentioned several times throughout the book but certainly bears repeating. The manner of Sgt. Ladner's death is no secret, given the incredible power of media and social networking. By sharing all the stories of and about Brandon Ladner's life, maybe another's will be affected. Maybe someone else's life will be saved.□

"I wanted my son's story to be known. If sharing Brandon's story saves just one other life, we will have accomplished what we set out to do."

-Renee

☐

-That Last Chapter Explanation:
'Why the First Chapter Became One of the Last'-

"The thing that makes life worth living is the possibility of experiencing now and then a perfect moment."

-Paul Bowles

"Humor is the world's best camouflage."
-DW, USN

How did the genuine first chapter actually become one of the last ones in this book? The whole point, after all, of this biographical account was to explain why the story of Marine Sergeant Brandon Ladner was so essential to share. It simply was not acceptable to begin Ladner's story with dozens of pages of explanation about all the quotes and blurbs (procured from many sources) that led to a unique combination of people working together to bring his story to light. In the words of Marine Staff Sergeant Nickomar Santana, "They all deserve to be remembered." This book was Brandon's story.

From Motorcycles to Machine Guns wasn't meant to be just about the charmed life of some Marine. It's an expressive portrait created from thousands of words: a painting coated with tremendous emotions shared by a veritable host of family, brother Marines, friends, and even people who were never blessed with actually knowing him. (Yeah, it's just like that.) Brandon's life became a serious lesson to be learned, one to be taught, one necessary not only because of the circumstances in which he died but more necessary because of how he lived.

"Don't become so busy that you start taking life for granted."

There's no subtle or delicate way to address the matter of Veteran suicide, no eloquent way to segue into the story of any Marine (or other service member) who has chosen to take his/her own life. Readers can only be told how the author came to know about Sergeant Brandon Charles Ladner in the first place.

In the nursing profession, if you don't chart a test, a dressing change, or whatever other procedure or action that's been ordered, then it wasn't done: plain and simple. And unless it has affected you personally, a death in the military doesn't have much (if any) emotional impact, or doesn't matter, didn't happen. Right or wrong, this seems to have been how the mindset of America turned, particularly after so many deaths were being reported on almost a nightly basis by various news agencies for so long. "Why should it matter to me? They volunteered to serve, they volunteered to go. Nobody forced them. What difference is it supposed to make to me?" The difference? You are free. You can read English, sleep peacefully, sing, assemble, speak, drive, go, and run for office; that's the difference, the difference it should make to us all. Freedom.

Sometimes before an entire story can be told, a little (or a lot of) information needs to be shared. Editors call such information backstory and generally tell their writers, *"Put it where it's needed."* With that being said, if you're not a military Veteran, you might want to go ahead and read this last chapter first. On the other hand, if you are a Veteran, (particularly a combat Marine or were blessed to have otherwise known or lived by Brandon Ladner), go back and start at the beginning.

Many have asked, "Of all the Marines who've taken their own lives, how was it that you happened upon Brandon Ladner's story specifically?" Answering that question was easy. There was another young Marine, a Lance Corporal by the name of David Baker, a man as tremendously loved by his family and friends as Brandon was by all of his, who provided the connection. Though these two Marines left this life under entirely different circumstances during two completely different points in time, they shared something in common. They both served with the Marine 1/5; 1st Battalion, 5th Marine Regiment 1st Marine Division on the same deployment. (You know, one of the groups of Marines who wear the braided green French Fourragère on their shoulders?)

I had interviewed dozens of Marines and Navy Corpsmen for a biographical project published about Baker several years back and had kept in contact with many of those same Veterans after his book was complete. (Incidentally, LCpl Baker was killed in action while walking point on a foot patrol in Afghanistan in October 2009.)

As has been mentioned before, Brandon's was not the first PTSD-related suicide suffered by his unit, nor was his the last. When news of his passing was so judiciously shared in various pop media outlets, I knew immediately that I wanted to know who this Marine was and what had happened in his life to have compelled him to choose to end it. I wanted to talk to his friends and family and learn about who he was before everything happened. I wanted to tell this Marine's story to the rest of the world.

In attempting to gather interviews that told the story of Brandon's life, the process became a matter of some effort. People were extremely hesitant to open themselves up to questions posed by somebody they'd never met about a matter still fresh in their hearts and memories. Despite the deadlines and numerous requests and shout-outs, relatively few stepped forward.

It was requested by Brandon's mother Renee that this poem, *'Hi, My Friend'* (written by Brandon's friend Kyle Scott) be included in this story.

-'Hi, My Friend'-
By Kyle Scott

Hi, my friend. How you doing, kicking it on the other side?
Looking down on me with a smile remembering those good old days back in 2002. I remember those days like it was yesterday, laughing, we were going crazy drinking liquor to make the time go by quicker; heart's racing.
When we were put into a corner, we had each other's backs;
Fists up. Ask questions later.

Hi, my friend. How you doing, kicking it on the other side?
Looking down on me with a smile remembering those good old days back in 2003. Do you remember the night we lived life on edge? Just driving all through the night; speeding, loud music, yelling, screaming, howling at the moon?
Couldn't tell right from wrong,
Just skipping our CD with the same old song.

Hi, my friend. How you doing, kicking it on the other side?
Looking down on me with a smile, remembering those good old days back in 2004. I remember this year best because we grew up, a little older but still had fun like we were still some kids.
Working jobs, trying to make a steady check, but we were both a wreck hating life and everything about it, so I moved away back home and left you all alone.

Hi, my friend. How you doing, kicking it on the other side?
Looking down on me with a smile,
Remembering those good old days back in 2006.
I came to visit. It was two years since we last hung out. We started
out with cold beers asking,
'How's it been going? How's life been treating you?'
'Life's been good.'
Talking about memories we'd never forget,
Our stories were legit and we never knew when to quit…

Hi, my friend. How you doing, kicking it on the other side?
Looking down on me with a smile, remembering the day you left us.
I was at work when I got the call from my brother.
I couldn't believe it, no it wasn't true.
I fell to my knees, screaming out to the sky asking why.
It was a lie that you died, now I'm mad as hell:
Punching the wall until I drank myself. Until I fall.

Hi, my friend. How you doing, kicking it on the other side?
Looking down on me with a smile,
Remembering those good old days.
It had been two years since I last visited.
Now I talk to you in a box with prayer,
About the old days because that's all we had.
I look up to the sky, say 'goodbye' and 'I love you my brother.'
Walking to my car, I start smiling,
Because of all those good old days we had.

Hi, my friend. How you doing kicking it on the other side?
Looking down on me with a smile
Remembering those good old days…

---☐

-His Own Words-
"That's cool man."

In April of 2016, author Fitzgerald once again took the opportunity to visit Alabama, meeting with the people and organizations preparing for the Rally and Roll event honoring Brandon's life. Looking through hundreds of photographs with Brandon's mother that day, there also came opportunity to read a few of the many letters that he wrote home while completing Marine Basic Training.

In addition to sharing the interview sessions of those who chose to step forward, here are just a few paragraphs written years ago by Brandon himself, which help demonstrate who he truly was. It may seem that perhaps there would be more to read, but these excerpts were copied from personal letters. Despite the fact that this was a story about a Marine the world lost too soon to a dreadful circumstance, there were still many things too special to share with the rest of the world: letters home to mama were some of those things. (It must be mentioned that Brandon saved every single letter his mother Rene ever wrote to him.)

"Dear Mom.

It's Sunday and I just finished combat training. Thursday we start the Crucible...

I miss you so much. I feel like I haven't seen you or been home in years. I'll be back soon, though. Things are really going good for me. I made the right choice by coming here to be who I am now. It's not until you come to the Marine Corps

that you realize how much you have and the value of those things. Mom, you've done the best job in the world at raising me because now it's all paying off.
Love, your Rudy."

"Dear Mom.
I hope this letter finds you doing as good as I am. I read your letter about me as a child and tears of memories rolled out. I couldn't help it. I can't believe that I am already 19, but I hate it. Most kids want to grow up fast, but not me. I want to come back home and snuggle with my mom like when I was young…"

It only seemed fitting to conclude the sharing of Sgt. Ladner's story with a note written by his mother…

"My Dearest Son,
You were always such an ambitious go-getter with so many goals. You accomplished many things and I was very proud of you. You would never allow me to be sad and were always making me laugh no matter what the situation or how I was feeling. I try to remember that's what you would want for me now. You felt you needed to fight your own battles alone and I am so sorry. I didn't know. I never realized that you were hurting like you were.
You always told me that I was the strongest woman you had ever known and would always assure me that everything would work itself out. I keep those words close to my heart and am trying to be that person for you. I struggle with losing you every day but I find comfort in knowing that I will see my little Moe again one day. I love you and miss you, my beautiful son."

As completion of this book neared, Brandon's mother Renee shared a note of thanks to various people and organizations:

"I want to thank each and every person who has stepped forward to help. Tremendous thanks to Mission22 for bringing much-needed awareness of PTSD and for their reaching out when we lost Brandon. A big thank-you to TM

Fitzgerald for her love and compassion for all Veterans. She made this book possible so we could get Brandon's story out with the hope that it may save other lives. "If we positively affect even just one life, then we have done what we set out to do." Pulling together all of the stories about Brandon's life with family and friends to read have truly given my family and I comfort through this sad journey we live daily since losing Brandon."

"Brandon was such a sweet, kind, thoughtful, loving, beautiful, funny child and friend. There is no greater loss than losing a child. Please tear out and use the pages included in this book and share with family and friends or with anybody who may be in the process of PTSD. You may very well save a life."

Brandon's Mama

-Leaving Ground; an Author's Aside-
October 15, 2016

Attempting to complete the process of putting together and publishing the biographical account of Brandon Ladner, I tried to execute all related tasks on significant dates: individual interview sessions, round-table discussions, meeting certain deadlines, etc. In the process, the actual completion of Brandon's story fell on what would have been his 29th birthday. However, it just so happened that the organization Mission22 had scheduled to dedicate it's *'War at Home'* memorial on Saturday, October 15th, 2016. Brandon's mother Renee invited me to travel with her to Bandera, Texas to attend the dedication and she wanted the moment to be part of Brandon's story. So, I made the familiar drive south of Birmingham to meet Renee and we were scheduled to leave the day.

There wasn't an empty seat on the plane that sunny afternoon. Quiet conversations took place as we sat waiting our turn to taxi down the runway. While we waited, I glanced around wondering how many passengers knew anything about the number twenty-two. While I sat thinking about our journey, people all around were busy with last minute banking, taking selfies or finishing up video games before being told to shut everything down. At 3 pm on October 14, we left the ground.

The flight to San Antonio was without event. We landed, hit the car-rental counter and were soon on our way to the River Walk in downtown San Antonio. Although there was a lot of foot traffic, we had arrived rather late in the evening and not many places were open. After walking around a little while, we were soon en route to Bandera, Texas; *"Cowboy Capital of the World."*

The memorial dedication was slated to officially begin at five that evening, but Renee and I decided to journey to the grounds ahead of time so as to beat the crowds. Our lodging was only two miles down the road so we arrived within minutes. (The actual town of Bandera was located just a few minutes down the road, but in the opposite direction. Renee and I had ventured into town, picked up some lunch and did a little exploring before we were making our way back to Purple Sage Road.)

It was amazing to see the number of people who turned out. There we were at this unassuming compound located seemingly in the middle of Nowhere, Texas, witnessing such support for the new Veteran treatment facility and memorial dedication. Upon arrival, families seemed immediately drawn to the circle of ten-foot tall, steel plated silhouettes arranged in front of the facility. With a mixture of sadness and pride, individuals who had made their way to the memorial started telling the story of their Veteran to anybody who paused to listen.

When it came time for the actual dedication ceremony, various family members stood at the microphone and lovingly talked about their Veteran. As the mother of one of the memorialized fallen, Renee had prepared words from her own broken heart to share:

> *"Good evening everybody. I am the mother of Marine Sergeant Brandon C. Ladner, one of the twenty silhouettes standing in this memorial. We lost my youngest son when he was twenty-seven years old on September 09th, 2014. Until that tragic day, our family had no idea what 'twenty-two a day' meant. When I received the phone call, I had no idea why or what could have possibly troubled my beautiful, loving son. "*
>
> *"Brandon was always the life of the party. He was so funny, intelligent, positive, motivated…he had such a bright future. He had already completed four years of college and was pursuing his Master's degree. Brandon worked seven days a week for the post office. He had so many goals in life, and he had already accomplished several of them in his twenty-seven short years.*
>
> *"The amazing organization Mission22 approached my family and me several months after we lost Brandon and asked if they could come to our home to talk about and share*

Brandon's story of how he lost his battle with PTSD at home. We were honored that they chose our Brandon for their documentary."

"Mission22, (along with so many others) has played a very big part in healing my broken heart. I will be forever grateful to all the people who have been part of my life since the loss of my beautiful son. I'll never let Brandon be forgotten.
Sincerely, Renee Lipsey and Family"

'The War at Home' memorial represents a deplorable statistic. Every day, twenty-two Veterans take their own life. Every day, a parent loses a child. Every day, another parent continues missing a child. In leaving Bandera, Texas the next morning, there was a bittersweet sense of accomplishment. Brandon Ladner was still making a difference with the life he lived.

☐

From Motorcycles to Machine Guns

-Additional Thanks and Acknowledgments-

Brandon Ladner's story would not be complete without specifically thanking and acknowledging a number of people who made this book possible.

First, thank you, Renee and Michael C. Ladner, for giving the world such an amazing man. The world was definitely a better place for having him in it.

Tremendous thanks go to each individual (whose names appear with their interviews in no particular order, by the way) who stepped forward and allowed the opportunity for interviews and roundtable discussions, people who each shared personal experiences with a world that will never get to meet, much less know Brandon Ladner, USMC.

Additional words of thanks go to Eric (and wife Carolyn) Fort (USMC) of the Lone Warriors whose assistance with Brandon's Honor and Remember Rally for PTSD goes beyond words. Thank you, Beirut Era Marine Kevin Ayres who directed me to the article about the Beirut Marine and 'Semper Fi'. Thank you to Alabama National Cemetery's director Quincy Whitehead, the Honor and Remember organization, Enewetak Atomic Clean-up Veteran Mark Sargent (USA) and son-in-law Chad Pulkkinen (and his employer Uni-Sim) for their wonderful contributions to the Honor and Remember presentation for Brandon on June 11th, 2016.

Thank you, Vinnie Accardi (Marine father) for title suggestions, and thank you to retired Marine Staff Sergeant Nickomar (and wife Shannon) Santana for their valuable input; to Brandon's Marine brother Cole Wilson who navigated through one of the final drafts of this manuscript, to Joel Doss, a childhood friend of Brandon's who was an integral part of the Honor and Remember Flag presentation, Kyle Scott (USMC) who allowed use of his writing, 'Hi, My Friend' to be shared in Brandon's story, Mr. Bob (and wife Barbara) Lipsey for sharing their home and hospitality post Rally and Remember event held in Brandon's honor, Travis Armenta (USMC) who unknowingly gave me several ideas which I incorporated in this book.

I thank my editor Bernie Weisz for making me strive to make this the 110% effort that I promised to all of Brandon's friends and family. I especially want to thank Sergeant Brandon Ladner for serving this country with the United States Marines and helping to protect my freedoms and rights and keeping us all free.

Memory: "Do you recall what a memory is?"
Person: "Sure I do."
Memory: "Well, do you remember me?"
Person: "Of course."
Memory: "Then can I stay for just a little while longer?"

-Make Your Life Spectacular-
Robin Williams, from the movie 'Jack'

You know, as we come to the end of this phase of our life,
We find ourselves trying to remember the good times
And trying to forget the bad times.
We find ourselves thinking about the future.
We start to worry, thinking, "What am I gonna do?
Where am I gonna be in ten years?"
But I say to you, Hey, look at me!
Please, don't worry so much.
Because in the end,
None of us have very long on this Earth.
Life is fleeting.
And if you're ever distressed, cast your eyes to the summer sky
When the stars are strung across the velvety night.
And when a shooting star streaks through the blackness,
Turning night into day...
Make a wish and think of me.
Make your life spectacular...
I know I did.

"If even a single person remembers you, then maybe you never really die at all."

-END-

Post-traumatic Stress Disorder (PTSD)
-Tear-and-Share-

"These pages appear again as a convenient way to keep PTSD information handy and accessible. Tear them out, post them on the fridge, or share with a friend. Reach out and help lift someone up."

-Fitzgerald

Post-traumatic stress disorder (PTSD) is a mental health condition triggered by experiencing or witnessing a terrifying event: ANY event. It could be war, rape, a near-death experience, ANY traumatic event. Symptoms may include (but are not limited to) flashbacks, nightmares and severe anxiety, as well as uncontrollable thoughts about the event. PTSD can be experienced by anyone: man, woman, child, civilian, military, etc. PTSD does not discriminate.

Many people who have experienced traumatic events have difficulty adjusting and coping for a while, but with time and good self-care, they usually get better. If the symptoms get worse or last for months or even years and interfere with daily functioning, then it may be PTSD. Post-traumatic stress disorder symptoms may start within three months of a traumatic event, but sometimes symptoms (which can cause significant problems in social or work situations and in relationships) may not appear until years following. Symptoms may include:

- Recurrent, unwanted distressing memories of traumatic event
- Reliving the event as if it were happening again (flashbacks)
- Upsetting dreams
- Severe emotional distress/physical reactions to things reminding person of the event
- Negative feelings
- Inability to experience positive emotions
- Feeling emotionally numb
- Lack of interest in once enjoyable activities
- Memory problems, including not remembering important aspects of the traumatic event
- Difficulty maintaining close relationships
- Changes in emotional reactions
- Irritability, angry outbursts or aggressive behavior
- Always on guard for danger

- Overwhelming guilt or shame
- Self-destructive behavior, such as drinking too much or driving too fast
- Trouble concentrating
- Trouble sleeping
- Being easily startled or frightened
- Intensity of symptoms

PTSD symptoms can vary in intensity over time and individuals may have more symptoms when he or she is stressed in general, or when they run into reminders of what they went through. For example, a Veteran may hear a car backfire and relive some traumatic combat experience or a woman may see a report on the news about a sexual assault and feel overcome by memories of her own assault.

If a person has disturbing thoughts and feelings about a traumatic event for more than a month, if they're severe, or if that person is having trouble getting his/her life back under control, encourage them to talk to a health care professional and get treatment as soon as possible to help prevent PTSD symptoms from getting worse.

If you or someone you know is having suicidal thoughts, get help right away. Reach out to a close friend or loved one.

- Call a suicide hotline number — in the United States, call the National Suicide Prevention Lifeline at 800-273-TALK (800-273-8255) to reach a trained counselor. Use that same number and press 1 to reach the Veterans Crisis Line.

If you know someone in danger of committing suicide or has made a suicide attempt, make sure someone stays with that person. Call 911 or the local emergency number immediately or take the person to the nearest hospital emergency room.

☐

ABOUT THE AUTHOR

TM Fitzgerald is a Veteran and Veteran's advocate who lives in the Midwestern United States. When her own anticipated life-time career in the military was unexpectedly cut short because of a repeat-offending, uninsured drunk driver, Fitzgerald determined to find a way to continue serving her country. With the various books and movies about famous generals, commanders and battles already available to the world, Fitzgerald decided she would attempt to give voice to and tell the stories of those who needed a hand or weren't able to tell their own. *"We all have a story to tell. But in the end, some of us deserve to be more than just a story..."*

www.ingramcontent.com/pod-product-compliance
Lightning Source LLC
Chambersburg PA
CBHW060241290526
45789CB00001B/143